Winding Road to Freedom

15 Entrepreneurs Share Their Journey to Financial Freedom

Inspired by Buck Flogging
Created and Orchestrated by Dustin Rusbarsky
Promotional Support by Derek Doepker

[Featuring 15 Financially Free Co-Authors]

This book does not have a copyright.

If you want to use someone's story, it's general courtesy to notify them first.

If you want to bless someone else with this book, it's general courtesy to purchase it for them.

That being said, you are free to make your own moralistic choices in this world.

Uncopyright 2016, Winding Road to Freedom

www.WindingRoadtoFreedom.com

Website, Ebook, Paperback, and Cover Design by Rusbarsky Custom Digital Products

This book is dedicated to all those who seek freedom in their lives.

May the words in this book touch your life.

Table of Contents

Introduction, *vii*

The Vision, *x*

Matt Stone: *An Accidental Entrepreneur,* **1**

Isabel Nicole Wong: *From Rejection, Ridicule, and Humiliation to Success, Happiness, and Freedom,* **18**

Kate McKibbin: *Starting from the Start,* **32**

Derek Doepker: *Why Everything's So Easy for Me,* **50**

Patrick King: *The Humble Beginnings Are What Truly Matter,* **63**

Andi Cumbo-Floyd: *From Professor to Portable Toilets to Farm-Life Bliss,* **76**

Bryan Cohen: *Presents, Passion, and Potholes,* **90**

Christopher Westra: *From Working in a Prison to Being Financially Free,* **101**

Dragos Roua: *3 Different Kinds of Freedom,* **114**

Henri Junttila: *From Passion to Purpose and Building Confidence,* **134**

Luke Jones: *The Foundations of Massive Success,* **155**

Paige Burkes: *The Winding Road to Happiness,* **177**

Rob Cubbon: *How to Get Laid,* **195**

Steve Mueller: *True Financial Freedom: It's NOT About Money*, *215*

Vidya Sury: *Outside the Comfort Zone is Where the Magic Happens!*, *227*

Afterword, *248*

Introduction

Money is a beautiful thing.

There's nothing wrong with having money...as long as it doesn't *have you.*

And even though this is a book about *financial* freedom, you'll quickly notice that for each one of the 15 coauthors in this book, money alone was not the focus.

Money is simply viewed as a tool and a metric for deeper, more meaningful goals.

Put simply, people want to be free.

Free to live life on their own terms

Free to pursue their passions and hobbies, without having to trade the majority of their lives to do so.

Free to overcome their limitations and live a life of self actualization.

And free to share their gifts with other people.

It is through the journey to freedom that we will be able to create a unified planet of peace and prosperity.

Given the liquidity of money in today's world, the prospect of financial freedom is a wonderful arena in which to explore all of the above goals.

At the end of the day, when each of us takes our last breath on this planet, we all want the same things. We want to know that we made a difference in other people's lives.

We want to know that we made the planet a better place.

And, as with any change you wish to see in the world, all successful endeavors begin with YOU.

What you will soon begin to notice is that these coauthors have created a lifestyle doing what they love while achieving increasing levels of abundance and influence to share with others and help make the world a better place.

That's what this book collaboration is all about.

Each of these 15 coauthors was selected based on their challenges and failures just as much as their breakthroughs and successes. They have willingly opened themselves up in a vulnerable way in order to help you, dear reader, embark on your own journey to financial freedom.

As you read these testimonies, try to keep the big picture in mind. Notice what each of these entrepreneurs have in common.

Although the winding road to freedom is unique for every individual, no one is exempt from things like failures, doubts, struggles, or insecurities.

This book can be used as a resource to help you realize that you are not alone…that no matter where you are in your journey to financial freedom (even if you're miles away from starting it), we've all been there.

The words in this book are a powerful reminder of the extraordinary connections we share in the human experience.

Let these words inspire you to take that first/next step, even if you don't yet know what that step is.

Any step will do, even if it's a step "backwards."

The stories these people will share with you will show you that mistakes and failures are not only a necessary feature of the journey, but should be welcomed with open arms.

By reading these testimonies, you will see how uncertainty and failure are actually the gateways to massive success.

So from all of us in *Winding Road to Freedom*, we wish you great failure on your journey, and the tenacity to never give up until you, too, experience massive success.

Freedom is yours for the taking…

…so reach out and grab it.

Sincerely,

The Winding Road to Freedom Team

The Vision

The Winding Road to Freedom movement goes so much further than just a book. Our vision is to help one million people achieve financial freedom for themselves and their families.

We believe that debt and poverty are two of the most harmful situations a human being can experience. And each person who becomes free can easily go on to save another ten thousand lives!

Our mission is **not** to help people become rich, but rather to *set them free* on a journey of financial independence.

To demonstrate this difference, imagine for a moment that you make $10,000 every month. Sounds pretty nice, doesn't it?

But what if you had to sacrifice your health, your friends, your family, and your ability to see the world and have unique experiences? Would you still do it?

On the flip side, imagine making $3,000 each month but being able to do what you wanted whenever you wanted. Imagine having the ability to scale your income as you learn new skills and expand your horizons. Imagine having no boss and getting to spend your time exactly how you see fit.

Just imagine for a moment being able to travel as you please, living in a place for only as long as you feel like. Feel how *free* that is?

What if you could go anywhere you want without ever having to worry about money? What if "money" became a game for you…what if you no longer **needed** it, and instead you just started *enjoying* it?

Now you tell me: would you rather be rich and enslaved or comfortable and free? Most people reading this book will choose the latter.

And if you're one of those people, we invite you to join this vision by going to WindingRoadtoFreedom.com and signing up for 100% free email updates that will accelerate *your* journey to financial freedom.

Matt Stone

Matt Stone started out as a passionate purist, doing extensive health and nutrition research and documenting it on his now inactive blog, www.180degreehealth.com, with no entrepreneurial interest or know-how whatsoever. His daddy literally had to do everything for him. Register a business name. Set up a business bank account. Set up payment processing. Find a web developer...you get the picture.

Speaking of pictures, Stone was such a digital newb that it took him two years just to figure out how to put an image into a blog post. Not the brightest bulb in the lamp folks.

Stone, perhaps the unlikeliest of entrepreneurs, actually garnered a large following online, published some books, and became a multiple bestselling author at the helm of a business generating *nearly $200,000 in sales annually...all without ever reading a single book about entrepreneurship, business, online marketing, or anything of the sort.*

He then launched www.buckbooks.net, which became more or less an overnight success that has gone on to make a few shockwaves in the publishing industry (while bringing in tens of thousands of dollars of monthly revenue within its first year). In fact, he recently launched a Buck Books event that earned him $70,000 in one day!

Seeing that these repeated successes weren't simply luck, Matt created QuitN6 to reveal the strategies, tactics, and knowledge that other unlikely entrepreneurs can use to make the leap to successful and sustainable self-employment online.

An Accidental Entrepreneur

Hi I'm Matt Stone, better known as "Buck Flogging." The Buck thing is a long story, but I've been encouraged to tell a long story, so I guess you're about to hear the whole thing!

My story is an interesting one for sure. It started as humbly as you can imagine, and, ten years later, I manage a team of seven full-time workers in several countries who run a half dozen websites hauling in as much as $100,000 in a good month.

Funny thing is though, it all happened more or less accidentally. I've never had any interest in business, entrepreneurship, or had any ambitions or aspirations to run a company or earn a lot of personal wealth. I've never read a single book on any of those subjects!

Before my successes online I was a globetrotting transient that was perfectly content to spend my life sleeping in a tent, shunning financial wealth. No really, my ex-girlfriend watched that *Into the Wild* movie and was freaked out about how identical Chris McCandless was to me. And even this past summer, with a business looking to make over $1 million this year, I still managed to spend a couple months camping out in a cargo trailer.

I'm so non-career oriented that I've never once held down a full-time job for an entire year, and turned down countless advancement opportunities when I actually did have to "work" for a living. This was prior to late 2010 when I finally escaped employment once and for all (knock on wood).

So, how did a hippie-ish gypsy hobo of a character end up with a mini internet empire? Let's go back to the beginning and retrace the whole thing. I think once you hear the entire story you'll be quite inspired to pursue making an internet-based income, and you'll KNOW that you can do it.

At 28 I was coming to the end of a phase. I had spent the prior decade trying to recreate my way to happiness. I travelled all over the world in search of some good outdoor recreation opportunities (skiing, backpacking, snorkeling, etc.), and when I did have to work to make ends meet (usually for about half the year), I worked at ski mountains or as a Wilderness Ranger for the U.S. Forest Service. The most "normal" job I ever had was managing a health food store in Maui (yes, Maui), but I didn't even make it a full year doing that!

What I found in my many years of trying to basically vacation my way to happiness is that even recreation gets old after a while. I've come to think that humans just aren't satisfied unless we are making progress in some way, and fulfilling our potential to make an impact on the lives of others somehow. I came across a guru who preached that gospel, and it awakened within me a desire to stop trying to avoid work and actually do something challenging and inspiring.

But I didn't know what to do exactly.

Overly enamored with the guru that gave me a jolt of energy to actually DO something with my life besides snorkel with sea turtles and work on my tan (his name is Dr. John DeMartini by the way—he's like stale pizza in that he's cheesy on the surface and rock solid underneath it), I felt an urge to follow in his footsteps. I was gonna change people's lives man!

This was late 2006, and mind you, I went to school for Creative Writing. I have like, a real degree from a University. I know right?

But my writing career had been very short-lived after school. I got a book deal before I had even graduated, but that book was a total flop. It only made a couple hundred bucks lifetime, and still to this day it sits in some lost corner on Amazon with one pitiful review. By my dad. Pretty easy to give up on a writing career with that kind of failure!

Still, I secretly yearned to write, and when a co-worker of mine told me about this thing called a "blog," I was all ears. I didn't even own a computer with a modem at the time! It was a 1996 Toshiba that I used to type stuff on, which I saved on a floppy disk for safekeeping!

And so, once I got my hands on a modern laptop (a Gateway, remember those?), I started a blog: yoursacredself.blogspot.com. It was started purely as a hobby.

I started writing some new agey self-improvement and deep thought type of articles, because I wanted to be just like DeMartini. That didn't last long because I'm not DeMartini. Instead I had to figure out who I was and what I could do.

As I reflected on it, I realized pretty quickly that I was really into health and nutrition. The reason I had moved to Maui in the first place was because it helped my asthma. I spent all of my disposable income on organic food and nutritional supplements. The only books I liked to read were about health and nutrition, and the only books I was able to actually finish and remember were books about that subject. This was something that went back as far as I could remember. Even as an 8-year old kid when my friends were eating neon cereals with fancy toys in them, I was picking my breakfast cereals based on their vitamin and mineral content on the label. Picture an 8-year old going down the breakfast cereal aisle and picking a jumbo box of *Total*. Shit tastes like wood shavings!

But I didn't have a degree in nutrition or anything like that. I hadn't even read that many books about it. Maybe four. But, like any arrogant, entitled white kid that grew up in the suburbs, I did have some strong opinions about it, and I thought my opinions were important. I felt that nutrition and health information had been basically hijacked by commercial interests, and I thought of myself as someone who could research it in an unbiased way and report my honest findings.

And so, that's how it began. I launched an "independent investigation" and spent the next seven years researching and writing about health and nutrition obsessively. And when I say obsessively, I mean OBSESSIVELY. I read over 300 books, thousands of articles, thousands of studies, communicated with hundreds of leading authorities, made 300+ videos, and wrote a few MILLION words on the subject in multiple blogs, over a dozen books, 6,500 personal blog comments (most of them long-winded, multi-paragraphed tirades), thousands of personal emails, and the list goes on.

And I enjoyed every minute of it. It was the most exhilarating thing I've ever done in my life. Mind you, I was never very good in academics or a nerd or intellectual in any way. Finding the right subject to study (one I was genuinely and deeply curious about), changed everything for me.

But to think that it was an overnight success story would be laughable. It wasn't. Only someone as obsessed with health and "unobsessed" with money would have endured the many years of failure that I did. These failures resulted in losing every penny I had, having to move back in with my mom for a while, and even getting dumped because my girlfriend thought I was a loser.

"Clearly what you're doing isn't working," she once said.

In the first year I made $0.

In the second year I made $0.

In the third year I wrote my first "book" that I sold for $19.95 (it was a sloppy unformatted 20,000-word pdf file that didn't even have a book cover) and started a monthly eZine that could be accessed for $97 a year. My yearly total was around $6,500.

In the fourth year I got up to $23,000, which was almost enough to pay my living expenses without going deeper into debt each month, but not enough to keep from getting tossed out onto the street by my then girlfriend (who had pretty high standards, as she was 7 years younger than me and was one of the highest-ranking government employees at her age in the entire country).

In the fifth year I made $40,000.

In the sixth year I had a breakthrough and made $90,000 and hired my first helper.

In the seventh year I had a huge year at $170,000, but more than half of that went to my assistant and to my affiliates, whom I gave 90% commission (because, you know, I don't care about money). Summarized like that it looks pretty good, but five years to get to around $3,000 a month is really brutal. Like I said, I wasn't doing it to make money. If I had been, I surely would have quit long before I reached the point of success.

Enough of the not-so-detailed overview. I want to tell you EXACTLY how I made my first business successful, and why I ended up more or less ditching it for bigger and better opportunities once I had.

For the first year all I did was write articles and post them on my blog. A typical day brought in 30 or so visitors, which I was pretty excited about (and shouldn't have been, that's a pathetic amount of traffic for a blog). I wrote my little musings once per week usually, and every now and then a comment would come in and I'd do a little dance.

After a year of that, and hardly any increase in traffic at all, someone with an audience found me. He read through a lot of my material and liked it. He eagerly shared my blog with his followers in a large Yahoo group. That day I got over 300 visitors to my site! It was really exciting, and my comments section started blowing up. Since it was a Yahoo discussion group, the members of the group as well as the moderator were all about discussion and debate. I went from getting 2-4 comments per post to more like 20-40, a tenfold increase overnight.

The cool thing is that after getting a spike in traffic from 30 to 300, my traffic levels didn't drop back down. That one little burst in traffic improved how Google indexed my site, and I started drawing in quite a bit of traffic. My traffic levels stabilized at this new plateau.

But I stayed stuck at this traffic level for another couple of years. By then I had changed the name of my site to "180DegreeHealth" and actually had my book and newsletter for sale. In the first year I hadn't made squat. Just $6,500 or so. My bank account was down to absolute nothing, and I was faced with a decision:

Make it work or get a job.

I chose to figure out how to make it work. Sadly, I don't think I ever would have been successful if it wasn't for the things desperation made me do.

As luck would have it, as I made the decision to figure out how to make things work or die trying, I was hit with a clue as to what might get me there. My traffic, which had been steady at 300 visitors per day for two solid years, suddenly jumped up to 1,580!

You see, I had been writing my articles on my own little one-man island and basically waiting for the world to discover my genius insights and dazzling writing and sense of humor. But they hadn't really. Sure, one person with an audience did, and that was very impactful, but I wasn't exactly a household name!

But suddenly my traffic rocketed up overnight, and I scrambled to figure out where it came from. Where did that big burst of traffic come from? Someone had left the 7th comment on the New York Times Well blog—an article written by none other than Michael Pollan—and linked to an article of mine challenging some of his basic assertions. My site was inundated with traffic for several days and once again stabilized at a permanently higher daily traffic level.

And so, in desperation, knowing I HAD to get people to my site or be forced to go back to work, I started obsessively leaving comments on other health and nutrition websites. I subscribed to about 100 blogs and refreshed my feed every few minutes all day, 10+ hours per day. Every time a new post came out, I tried to quickly be the first to comment on the post, often with a confrontational remark and often with a link back to one of my articles discussing the very same topic. Within 30 days I had my traffic up over 1,000 visitors per day and was making over $2,000 per month—just enough to get by without having to go to work.

Not only that, but huge bloggers were posting articles about me. I was invited to several major podcasts, I received guest post requests, and I burst onto the alternative health and nutrition scene as a controversial figure that people just couldn't stop talking about.

And that's basically how I was able to finally reach the point of supporting myself financially without having to go to work anymore. It wasn't easy and it wasn't glamorous at all. I had no idea what I was doing really, and because of that I used a silly tactic to publicize my work. But with my back pressed against the wall I found a way and I made it happen. It was a major milestone in my life. Maybe the ONLY milestone in my life!

That was 2010, and I kept going and going all the way through 2013, basically doubling my revenue every year as my traffic soared to over 5,000 daily visitors.

But by that point, I was getting tired of the subject. Also, in the process of doing a bunch of weird dietary experiments (eating only meat for a month, consuming only milk for a month, force-feeding 40 pounds of blubber onto my body intentionally in 90 days), I had become a fatass and couldn't shake the weight (and actually gained even more trying to lose it), which was very humbling. My naïve aspirations of really arriving at some kind of earth shattering conclusion with my independent investigation and becoming a major public icon in the field had slipped away. I just lost my mojo, was no longer comfortable being on camera or speaking in public, and knew that the end of my health and nutrition career was already beginning.

Paired with waning interest in health was some degree of frustration with how I had set up my original business. I knew there were better ways to make a lot more money with less blood, sweat, and tears. And I knew success didn't have to take five years. I knew it because I had observed dozens of major successes amongst many of my peers, and many of the biggest successes were the quickest successes.

If there was one thing I had learned in my experience up to that point, it was that success came quick and easy when you could tap into the years of laborious audience-building work of others. I mean, I blogged my little fingers down to the bone and hardly got anywhere in three full years, but 30 days of showing up in front of other people's audiences put me on the map.

I had seen the same thing for others who found innovative ways to get other big authorities together to promote their work. The first I observed was an online summit created by a guy named Kevin Gianni. He interviewed a lot of big experts and got them all to promote his summit. He got something like 80,000 email subscribers in a week. At the time I had blogged for four years and only had around 2,000!

And that leads me to another important lesson that I had learned that inspired me to design a website and business totally differently, and that's the power of getting someone actually onto your email list where you can communicate with them repeatedly on your terms. At peak while blogging, I was getting 5,000 visitors to the site per day but only getting 10 email subscribers! Contrast that to today, and I'm getting more like 2,500 email subscribers on that kind of traffic with the better websites I've built, but let's not get too far ahead here.

Those lessons combined gave me disdain for blah blah blogging, and thus the character Buck Flogging (as in Fuck Blogging) was born. It was a perfect goofy pen name for someone who still relied upon my health and nutrition site income and couldn't suddenly and openly make a huge left turn into a new niche.

And so, armed with knowledge and experience, I set out to create something better than my original site.

The first site I built was with my first hired help, a guy named Rob Archangel. That's really his name!

Rob helped me get my books published on Amazon, Createspace, and Audible, and in the process really learned all the things it takes to publish on these platforms. I didn't have to do anything (well, that's not entirely true as I did narrate my books for Audible), and I found this to be quite a luxury. I was like, "Dude, you should think about providing this as a service to people like me."

So we discussed it and put it out there.

Did it take us five years to get it earning some decent money? No. It didn't even take us five months. It was almost instant. How did we do it? It was quite simple really…

I had learned the power of networking with other influencers in a niche, and so that's exactly what I did right from the start. I reached out to three of the biggest authorities in the self-publishing world and offered up our services to them. We did a good job, those authorities made considerably more money (by getting their books into other formats, like paperback and audiobook), and they in turn were more than happy to tell their audiences about the difference we had made for them, endorsing us as the go-to source for those services to tens of thousands of authors.

Six months in we were banking 5-figures a month and changed up our business model to more of a traditional publisher model (where we did the full works on each title and kept a portion of the royalties instead of charging for our services). This would ultimately prove to be a mistake that Rob abandoned within a year, but fortunately there were enough a la carte clients to keep poor Rob from getting buried financially.

Even more fortunately, the switch to a traditional publisher model motivated us to find a marketing solution to sell all these books we were publishing. I quickly came up with the idea for Buck Books (www.buckbooks.net), and I, along with my girlfriend and recently-acquired web development guy, slapped a site together in four hours.

The idea behind Buck Books was that it made for a good launch platform for our books. The going tactic in self-publishing at the time (and still to this day), is to release a book cheap to try to get as many paid downloads and reviews as possible in the first week or so. This makes the book more viable on Kindle when you switch to selling it at a higher price. So with Buck Books the plan was to build a list of subscribers and give them great deals on books so they would never have to "pay more than a BUCK for a BOOK ever again." It was good for the subscriber, good for our authors, and good for us.

A couple weeks later I had quickly put together our first discount book event. What I did is get 15 authors to drop the Kindle price of their books to 99 cents and all drive traffic to the same page where these books were featured. If 15 authors send, say, 1,000 clicks each to the page, then 15,000 visitors will see the sale, many of them scooping up multiple titles—leading to more book sales for every participating author. That was the idea. And it worked.

The idea was certainly not mine. I had seen a guy named Bryan Cohen do this. The difference was I actually paid the contributors a little bit to drive traffic (which encouraged participation), and I optimized the page to get email subscribers, both of which he had failed to do.

That event sent three books into the top #100 in the entire Kindle store, one of them mine! I gathered up a couple thousand email subscribers in just 48 hours, and the first month I raked in $1,600. It took me nearly 40 months of blogging before I had my first $1,600 month, and here I hit it right away!

I still didn't really know what I had in Buck Books. By the third month I was making over $3,000 and already starting to brag about the success. And then it jumped to $8,000 per month. I appeared on Chris Guthrie's podcast and talked about how blown away I was that it was hauling in so much money. Little did I know that after hiring someone to build bigger and better events to gather subscribers along with a couple of other small tweaks, that I'd make $35,000 with Buck Books just three months later! That's right, it was hauling in over $1,000 per day by just the seventh month. It was making double of what Archangel Ink (Rob's publishing company) was making, and I turned my focus on it.

Unfortunately, our ability to get subscribers kind of stalled out the following year. While we did manage to build a list of around 40,000 and do another $35,000 month in May at the 1-year point, we realized that there was something fundamentally flawed with our approach. And because I had geared up for growth up to $100,000 per month and beyond by building out a huge team and increasing our affiliate commission substantially, we actually found ourselves in a pretty tight financial squeeze.

I wasn't and am still not too bothered by low profits though. When you are trying to grow at all costs, profit doesn't much matter. It all gets absorbed back into the business to grow revenue. And I do that, not because of greed, but because once you are making enough money to not have to go to work anymore, and assuming you are not a materialist that's been brainwashed by our consumerist society (you can almost picture me climbing up on a soapbox to rant about this), it becomes more like playing a game. You want to go for a new high score. That's how it's been for me at least.

And, with a variety of new sites and new things we tested out, we made over $90,000 in revenue for three straight months to start 2016.

People thought I was crazy in 2013 to neglect a site making $170,000 a year to build something from scratch. But doing that led to more revenue in 2014.

Then in 2015 we neglected a site making $35,000 a month to work on projects that would collectively bring in more than $90,000/month just eight months later.

Funny thing is, in neglecting Buck Books we stumbled on some things that fixed our Buck Books problem—mainly figuring out a better way to grow our email list. I'm currently diving back into Buck Books and putting half of my team's emphasis on it.

I expect to get more email subscribers in the first month than we got for Buck Books in the first 30 months, and, if our past numbers are any indication, we should easily blow the lid off of the $100,000 ceiling with Buck Books alone (we have many other sites hauling in money each month in addition to Buck Books).

And that's basically my journey to success for my first ten years as an accidental entrepreneur.

I think my success can easily be summarized into a simple 5-step process that anyone can apply to achieve their own dreams of an internet-based income (what I call "Digital Freedom"):

1. Start
2. Keep going
3. Pay attention to what other people are doing successfully
4. Try a lot of things out and learn from what does and doesn't work
5. Make adjustments, focusing narrowly on what works and ditching what doesn't in the pursuit of perpetual growth and improvement

You can do that right? Yes of course. The more important question is, will you?

If you'd like more insights from me on how to build a successful internet business, and build it quickly using my quick-start methods, take my comprehensive, detailed course called Quit Your Job in 6 Months (QuitN6 for short).

You probably can't afford it though because you know I'm all about charging people a ton of money so I can save up for more boats n' hoes!

Kidding. In fact, you can select your own price. To find out more about it, just go to: www.QuitN6.com.

Isabel Nicole Wong

Isabel Nicole Wong, age 22 is the founder of Empowereign. She started her digital publishing business because she believes in creating something out of nothing and impacting the world with her creations.

Today, Empowereign has worked with over hundreds of thousands of clients from all over the world and continuing its mission of impacting the lives of 1 million individuals. Her mission is to empower each unique individual to be extraordinary and discover their potential to reign in life.

From Rejection, Ridicule, and Humiliation to Success, Happiness, and Freedom

A wanderlust at heart, Isabel enjoys travelling around the world and living a flexible lifestyle of working anytime and anywhere. The ability to be untethered to time and space while working was a blessing for her as this freedom is congruent to her unrestrained personality and the yearn for financial independence.

But here's the thing – things were not always like this for her. Most people only had the chance to see the glamour of her success which includes travelling around the world, enjoying time freedom and doing the things she loves anytime she wants.

While that is true, the glamour is merely a superficial façade. What people fail to see is that things were not always a bed of roses for Isabel. She was not born with a silver spoon where opportunities are aplenty. Hence, she had to work doubly hard to achieve what she envisioned for herself.

Underneath her glamour lie many shattered pieces of hopes and dreams that almost consumed her resilience and ambition to succeed. Moreover, she was charting an almost deserted territory where there were no clear route and instructions to guide her when she was still grappling with repeated failures and groping helplessly in the dark for help.

There are three major hard-knocks in her life which defined her and made her who she is today.

Her Rough Start

Isabel dropped out of school at the age of 16 because she was driven by an overwhelming desire to start her own business like her mentor. Isabel was drawn to the whole concept of entrepreneurship as it carries with it the fantasy of becoming a master of one's universe and dictating a lifestyle that knows no bounds.

Besides, Isabel saw entrepreneurship as an effective means to escape the reality of the endless paper chase. She saw little or no value in academic pursuits. She found it aimless and meaningless when the conventional academic route provided little to no direct application to the demands of the real-world. This is now becoming evident in the growing skills gap that many graduates faced despite being armed with a paper qualification that was originally thought to be a passport to the safe haven of job security and financial abundance.

With this in mind, it was no wonder that Isabel never came to terms with the value of schooling despite being fed and impressed on her with the herd mentality that school is the best place to receive education and guaranteed gateway to success. Besides, motivation was something that had always eluded her and this was especially so when her school teachers would mock her for being stupid and lazy. Isabel was solely judged based on her academic performance and was discarded as a hopeless individual and simply, a blemish on the school track record.

Being born into a conservative Asian family, her mom invested heavily in her to provide her with the best tuition and education. Isabel understood that her family meant well but her interest in her studies was nothing more than a flickering flame.

As if stuck in a broken record that repeats itself, this was a scenario that never changed throughout her 10 years of formal education. Her results were still rock bottom and at the end of every "Meet the Parent" session with her teachers, her teachers would nod their head in unison and agree that "Isabel will never make it in life".

Perhaps the only vivid memory of her schooling life was when the teacher who taught her Principle of Accounts shouted at her from the fourth floor in class and demanded her to go to the courtyard and sit under the hot sun for 30 minutes. She was a student counselor that was easily identified by the characteristic tie around her neck and could only wallow in humiliation and shame for her underperformance and lack of exemplary conduct as students passed by and looked at her quizzically. There were countless incidents and punishments that were dished out to her for being the least favorite student which ultimately boiled down to the intention of shaming and humiliating her. So school was pretty much it for 10 years.

At the age of 16, she took a major national exam but fared badly for it. She was rejected from most tertiary institutions and was automatically allocated to a course- Diploma in Customer Service- in a school with a notorious reputation. It was an endless cycle of rejections and dejections. She felt indignant that she was put through a system where her aptitude was measured against a yardstick that was broken and inaccurate. Throughout those 10 years of education, she did not manage to get into the school of her choice. Nothing was going her way. She felt like a complete loser.

In Asian societies, she would typically be labeled as a failure because of her inability and blatant disinterest to perform well academically. To others, a dismal result in national examination probably spells the end for her. In short, her destiny seemed sealed and doomed.

Her teachers' words resonated in her like a prophecy that is coming true.

At that point in her life, her mentor introduced her to a book titled "Rich Dad Poor Dad" by Robert Kiyosaki. She was amazed by it. She finally had a spark of inspiration and realized there was more to life than just being in the conventional education system. The book smashed all her pre-conceived beliefs about education and life.

And that was how the journey began…

The Gap Year

An intense cold war erupted between her parents, uncle and her when she revealed that she wanted to drop out of school; distant relationships that she had to grapple with at the tender age of 16 lasted for almost a year. Her parents were concerned but Isabel was stubborn and believed that the one-year would prove her worth.

During that period, her parents and uncle were very sarcastic and frequently made awful comments about her being an entrepreneur. In hindsight, they could not be entirely blamed for harboring such perspective when statistic had clearly shown that 90% of startups fail. But what differentiated Isabel from them was that she strongly believed she belonged to the 10% that had the potential to reign in life.

At 16, Isabel was adamant to make something out of herself. However, what pained her most was that the people who were dear to her not only doubted her ability but also made a mockery out of her. It created an emotional turmoil that remained indelible and almost destroyed her and her dreams.

When she created her first company after much deliberation, her uncle was everything else but congratulatory. He said "Please don't call yourself a boss. I took a long time to climb up the corporate ladder. Do not take things lightly and be so arrogant." It was her very first milestone as a budding entrepreneur but the celebration was short-lived and curtailed prematurely. Looking back, Isabel admitted that she was rather naïve to think that starting a business from scratch is very simple. But at the same time, she was hurt by the awful and haunting remarks made by her uncle that nearly trampled her dream.

Isabel's parents eventually relented and conceded to give her a grace period of one year to succeed in her business. Otherwise, she would be sent back to school.

During the gap year, she tried selling t-shirts, creating website and videos for companies and even spoke at an education conference in front of a crowd of 400 individuals.

In the education conference, she proudly declared to the crowd that her dream was to become a self-made millionaire by the age of 19. She was so psyched up about her goal that she even filled up an entire notebook of 200 pages by handwriting it with the sentence "I will become a self-made millionaire by 19." She was relentless about hitting her first million and at that time, she was all about being a millionaire.

What the audience and she did not know was how she was going to achieve her first million-dollar. She had no blueprint but a sketchy dream of success. Even though she spoke to a crowd about her dreams, she was still unclear as to how she was going to achieve her first million-dollar goal. She was still bumping around like a headless chicken without clarity or a clear plan of how she was going to get there.

What's Next, Isabel?

Feeling lost, stuck and confused, her mentors brought her over to a Digital publishing company where she worked as an intern and partner to sell products in the digital space. She spent 14 hours a day working on the product launch, and the office became her second home for the next 6 months. She was exhausted but driven to succeed.

So she worked, ate and slept in the office creating her first product and praying that her effort would eventually pay off and multiplies itself over.

6 months later…her product launch bombed - it was a complete flop.

She had 0 sales. 0 after 6 months of hustling.

She thought it might have been a technical glitch so she kept refreshing her inbox.

But again, 0 - nothing new popped up.

It was then when reality sets in and reared its ugly head that made her come to her realization that her one-year timeline was already up.

She failed – game over.

Judgment Day

It was 18 December 2011, Sunday.

She could still clearly remember sitting in a circle with her mentors and parents. Ironically, it was also the day where everything comes full circle – back to where she first started.

Nothing.

Reluctantly, she presented a review of her gap year outlining her failed attempts. A quiet disapproval hung in the air as her mentors and parents were not too pleased with her results.

She was then asked to leave the room.

A general consensus was made to send her back to school to continue her pursuit for a diploma like everyone else. In that instant, she felt that her gap year which acted like a refuge for her to escape the ruthless reality was suddenly wrenched away from her mercilessly.

Her thoughts ran erratically and without directions. Exactly one year before, she was an ambitious entrepreneur-wannabe. Now, she felt that her dream to become an entrepreneur was outright ridiculous.

And maybe her uncle was right about her.

Maybe her teachers were right about her that she would never make it in life.

Maybe she was wrong about her own abilities and aptitude all along.

Maybe she was drawn to entrepreneurship like a moth to a flame.

Maybe it was nothing but wishful thinking.

As these self-deprecating thoughts overwhelmed her and started consuming her from the inside, she tried so hard to fight back her tears. Her strong demeanor could no longer hold up to the gravity of her failure. Tears swelled up and no amount of blinking could withstand the prolonged build-up of disappointment, embarrassment and hopelessness.

It was just too much for her to take.

She ran.

She burst through the doors and started jumping down the stairs and ran as fast as she could because she wanted to hide from everyone even if it meant only a few minutes.

She needed to be alone with herself.

Her mentors and parents chased after her in their cars searching for her.

She saw her dad running and shouting out to her from the back and she ran even faster.

The next thing she heard was the screeching of the car tire.

It was such a dramatic moment that her dad was almost knocked down by a car.

She shivered in fear and rejection and became too weak to fight the inevitable. So she stopped resisting the mainstream education that everyone is trying to shove down her throat.

Her three major hard-knocks are as follow: Firstly, her teachers in school had completely given up on her. Secondly, her mentors put a dream in her and crushed it into pieces. Thirdly, she was regarded as a complete embarrassment and a laughing stock for boasting to all her friends that she would become a millionaire within that gap year only to be sent back to school.

She felt like the world gave up entirely on her. She was completely vulnerable and she hated her own existence. Drowned in humiliation and feeling like the lowest life-form on Earth, she dragged herself back to school.

When she was in school, she insisted on continuing her Internet venture as she still believed that she was able to accomplish something that can prove her worth. She saw a glimmer of hope in herself when nobody else sees it.

The Turning Point

When she regained her composure and loosened the emotional attachment of failing, she reflected and found that the primary reason her venture flopped was that she had no solid execution plan. Benjamin Franklin's words "If you fail to plan, you plan to fail." rang true. In that instant, she learnt the full meaning and bears the full brunt of the consequences in the hardest way possible. But if not for this self-reflection and interrogative introspection, she would not have been able to pinpoint her mistakes, move on and improve herself.

After realizing this and coming to terms with her past failures, she reconciled with herself and rekindled her passion. Every day, she would lock herself up in her room to work on her online business. To brush up on her skills, she invested her pocket money on many courses online to learn as much as she can…

On average, Isabel worked almost 15 hours every day just to launch a product. Ideally, there would be a team of people armed with their own set of expertise to work on a product. This would greatly expedite the process of product launch. However, Isabel's circumstances were different. Nobody believed in her dreams and therefore, finding a partner to work alongside her for something that may not have a definite positive outcome was almost impossible and unimaginable. So, Isabel slogged away by herself but held on tightly to her battered dreams.

Every day, she emailed over 1000 prospects just to get one person to respond and support her launch.

It was a waiting game filled with anticipation and anxiety that led to many sleepless nights and loss of appetite for several weeks. Basically, Isabel lived and breathed her venture every day. For her venture, she was willing to sacrifice the time for her friends and movies – pastimes that were typical and defining of an adolescent's life. Instead, she worked tirelessly at her own product but was never overcome by exhaustion.

Finally, one day a breakthrough came when someone with a huge database agreed to mail for her launch. The rest is history.

Regardless of any circumstance, Isabel believes that everyone possessed the gift of the power of choice.

Isabel believes that, in any given moment, we get to choose how we are going to feel or how we are going to react to things. For Isabel, she chose to continue the pursuit of her dreams while her friends were all partying and having fun in school and went home every day after her lessons to work on her business. She was glad and heartened that her sacrifices finally came to fruition. Additionally, she would always be grateful for the generosity of the person who came forth to support her launch out of the many thousands of people whom she had reached out.

That was her first baby step in the internet marketing space.

Her determination stems from her desire to not be deemed as a failure. In her perspective, all she wanted to do was to prove to everyone that she can make it with her own ability.

3 greatest lessons from her journey:

1. Reframe your mindset
While it is important to possess the right mindset in order to succeed, it is good to dream big. There will always be objections and rejections along the way but that is only part of the journey.

The greatest battle is not fought with others but within yourself. If you are convinced and believed in your own ability to accomplish what you set out to achieve, then you have nothing to worry about – not even the dirtiest look or the nastiest comment others might give you.

2. Gain absolute clarity
As Isabel had shared earlier, she was once disillusioned and masked by her ambitious dream. One key take away from her story is that you have to be absolutely clear about what you want to achieve otherwise you will end up being busy doing things that have no tangible consequence and might possibly derail you from your intended destination.

3. Plan
As with any other businesses, there has to be a concrete plan and timeline. It is not enough to tell others that you have a dream. But it is equally important to break down your goal into manageable sub-goals. Schedule your time properly to effectively achieve these sub-goals. Before you know it, you would be one step closer to your goal.

Of course, it was impossible to connect the dots looking forward when she was in her gap year but it was crystal clear looking backwards 5 years later. The late Steve Jobs, founder of Apple Inc once said "Again, you can't connect the dots looking forward; you can only connect them looking backwards. So you have to trust that the dots will somehow connect in your future. You have to trust in something - your gut, destiny, life, karma, whatever. This approach has never let her down, and it has made all the difference in her life."

In summary, Isabel is thankful for the success of her Internet business that enabled her to travel, live her dreams while working on her business.

Do not set the limits and listen to the naysayers that put your dreams down. Believe in yourself and your potential.

Kate McKibbin

Kate McKibbin is a very-tall, super nerdy pun-enthusiast who, after cutting her teeth in the magazine industry, in 2007 launched one of Australia's largest independent lifestyle blogs (Drop Dead Gorgeous Daily), and has several awards and a team of lovely staff to show for her efforts.

In 2014 Kate created her second business, Secret Bloggers' Business (www.secretbloggersbusiness.com) to share everything she has learned about how to create, grow and run a successful blogging business. Kate has so far taught over 1000 bloggers how to turn their passions into a profitable business and it is her mission to have helped 500 bloggers to make at $5000 a month or more from their blogs in the next 5 years.

Starting from the Start

I guess if I'm going to share my story, I really should start at the start.

And my start was growing up in a very small country town in Victoria, Australia (my primary school had less than 50 kids in it when I was there), with not a whole lot of money, and very little to do (translation: I spent most of my childhood bored out of my mind by the small town I lived in, and counting down the days until I could run away so the fun part of my life could start!).

We were never properly "poor"; we had a house and food. But we weren't really "well-off" either.

And I remember there being stages where I just knew money was tight. So I would fail to tell my parents about things like school camps or dances, because I didn't want to make things any harder for them.

I also remember knowing, from a very young age, that I would have my own business one day, probably because my dad had a small business of his own. Or maybe because I hate being told what to do. Maybe it was a combo, who knows.

It was just always a fact, and I was just waiting for the right idea to come along.

Now growing up I wasn't the brightest kid, above average probably, but nothing scholastically special. But I was always the kid with the big dreams and the big ideas. And I always remember knowing (once I got past my initial stage of wanting to be a dolphin-training-kinder-teacher with her own jewelry store on the side), that I didn't want to waste my life on doing something small, expected or boring.

I wanted to lead a big, exciting life.

One that was the exact opposite of my small-town country life, where most people dropped out of school as soon as they could to get a low paying job and have babies.

Not that there is anything wrong with that, but I wanted something more.

And I guess some things never change.

Project Shoe Money

Now fast-forward to a 25-year-old (and already on, and bored of, her second career) me.

I was working as the online editor/writer for one of Australia's leading fashion magazines. And despite having achieved what I had been previously told was impossible, getting one of the most sought after jobs in the country.

"The dream job"

I am once again feeling restless. That I wanted more.

I was also feeling very broke (it is appalling how little the well educated and insanely hard working people in publishing are paid by the way, but that's a whole different story).

I spent my days drooling over and writing about luxurious experiences, homes, restaurants, holidays, shoes and other beautiful things. But I had to work part time on the weekends at a pet store to be able to afford my rent.

Yep, I was a super glamorous fashion journalist, who shoveled puppy sh*t on weekends so she could afford to buy shoes from Target.

So basically, I was 25, bored, broke and without a single responsibility (aka nothing to lose!).

There couldn't have been a more perfect time for me to finally stumble upon that "big idea" that I had been waiting for.

Well, my first one anyway.

The idea actually came to me as something I wanted to try on the website I ran for my day-job.

Online shopping was just starting to hit Australia (it was 2007), and as I wrote for a magazine that was all about shopping, I thought why not make our website all about ONLINE shopping.

It made sense to me, but my boss wasn't so keen.

I however had fallen in love with the idea, and once they passed on it decided to (with their blessing of course), give it a go myself.

I mean why not, right? As I said I had nothing to lose.

Plus it was the perfect combo of all my previous work experience, and I was a natural born nerd (I had designed my first website at the age of 14), so I could DIY pretty much everything I need to get started.

This was the birth of my very first business, Drop Dead Gorgeous Daily.

A business that I started as a little side project to hopefully earn some extra "shoe money" as I called it, and ended up being an award-winning business that I quit my job 12-months later to run full-time, and grew to have half a million monthly visitors and a team of five.

Not So Happily Ever After

And that probably sounds like the "fairy-tale" business story, right?

Everything was rubbish, and then you have that light bulb moment, and boom!

Your business is an overnight success, your bank account starts over-flowing and all your problems magically disappear, right?

Well I hate to tell you, but that is the exact opposite of the truth.

Yes, I did create a business that turned over a decent amount of money.

That grew really quickly, and that managed to succeed when most others in that same industry were failing.

But this is my story of finding financial freedom.

And in fact in this particular business, what I found was constant stress, struggle and barely making ends meet month after month.

I also found a lot of priceless business and life lessons, and an unmatchable amount of personal growth which I will be forever grateful for (more on that later).

But at the time, stuck in the middle of it, it seemed that no matter how hard I worked, or how many sales I made, I could never really get ahead. And while yes I was paying myself more than I could have earned in my previous job, I also was working 7 days a week, often late into the night (or early into the morning, depending on how you look at it).

And if you sat down and worked out what my hourly rate was, well I probably could have earned more working the fry station at MacDonald's.

I also have to add that in this business my main job was basically being a combo of tech-support and a cold-calling ad sales rep, while my team got to do all the fun stuff. And it was killing my creative soul each and every day.

I was so stressed and unhappy at one point that I started sleep walking, and I would wake up to find myself sitting at my desk, slumped over my computer most nights.

Meanwhile I was being celebrated left and right for being such a success.

But in reality I was 31, miserable, getting divorced, gaining weight, and totally trapped by my business.

Overcoming the BS

Right, now before you pull out the tiny violins.

I am not sharing any of this to get your sympathy.

Rather I want to show you what is so often the case behind the smiling, shiny pictures shared on social media.

The truth is, a lot of small business owners, particularly those in their first business, have absolutely no idea what they are doing.

Myself included.

I had a Business degree, but no "running a *small* business" experience.

I could tell you how to create multi-million dollar marketing campaigns, and what to do to protect your manufacturing patent. But I had no idea how to create a small business that would support me in the ways that I wanted. Or give me the lifestyle I desired.

In fact I didn't even realize that was even an option!

And, as is the case with some many entrepreneurs, I ended up creating a business that wasn't really a business at all, but a rather badly paid job with unreasonable hours and horrible benefits.

Which is all kinds of crazy when you think about it.

Because most people (myself included) go into business for themselves for one reason: *Freedom.*

Freedom to do what we want, when we want, where we want, how we want, with whomever we want.

But unless you actually actively set up your business to allow you to do that, then it usually will do the exact opposite.

And as you can see, I had to learn this the hard way.

More damn light bulbs

Now roughly around this time of hitting my breaking point, I was lucky enough to have been treated to an amazing (and unexpectedly life-changing) massage by a close friend.

And it was while lying face-down on that table for almost two hours, with nothing but my thoughts for company that I finally acknowledged the mess I was in.

Previously through a combination of extreme stubbornness and ego I had just been ignoring it (I did the same thing with my marriage).

I always felt like I was just one small win away from cresting the wave and things finally becoming easy.

But staring at that ornamental bowl of floating jasmine petals through the face-hole I couldn't deny it any more.

My business didn't work *for me*.

Sure it worked.

It made money, it was growing, and people really liked it.

But it wasn't right for me.

And if I wanted things to change in my life, then my business had to change along with it.

Drastically.

Just push, push, pushing was not going to solve anything.

And then, once again, right at that moment where I once again had nothing to lose, a new idea came to me.

One that I realized had been floating around at the back of my head for years, but I wasn't willing to listen to it until now.

There are easier ways to make money.

Now, as you have probably noticed, I am not one to sugar coat things.

So I won't here either.

The idea that popped into my head that day, while I was having 5-years worth of laptop abuse kneaded out of my back was nothing revolutionary.

And that's probably why I had been avoiding it for so long.

Because you see it turns out there were three BS (that's short for Bull Sh*t for the non-potty-mouths reading this) subconscious stories I had been telling myself pretty much my whole life.

And not only were they were a big part of the reason I had ended up in the mess I was in.

They were also *not* true.

And it was finally identifying these stories that had been holding me back for so long (and doing a lot of personal work on silencing them), that really helped me to go from an over-worked, under-paid, wrung-out business owner, to a happy, healthy and on-my-way-to-wealthy one who loves their business (most days!).

BS Myth 1 – You have to do something totally unique for it to be a "real" success.

I am not sure where this myth came from, probably from spending my life idolizing people like Steve Jobs and his whole "think different" mantra.

I really did seem to think to be "successful" you had to come up with something totally brand-spanking new.

Something no one had ever done or thought about before.

And that there was little to no merit in taking an existing (aka proven), business model and making it your own or improving it.

That was just cheating, or stealing, so why bother (or that is what I told myself anyway).

So I always pushed against doing the things that everyone was doing, and in turn then ended up doing everything the hard way (because there is normally a reason everyone is doing the thing that everyone else is doing. It works!).

BS 2 – *Success isn't and shouldn't be easy aka easy success = bad!*

This one, unsurprisingly, I learnt from watching my dad.

Not blaming him at all, he is a very hard-working, successful and wonderful man.

And his amazing work ethic is definitely one of my better traits.

But it's weird the way a small child's brain works.

As I was watching my dad start and grow his business - and then even once his business was up and running and doing really well - it always just seemed like such hard work.

So I clearly put the two together, and became almost distrustful of anything that seemed "easy".

Or even just *easier*.

Now of course all businesses require hard work and hustle.

But some definitely more than others.

And what I have learnt from my second business (and also planning my third) is that if you set your business up right, then it becomes the quality of the hustle (not the quantity) that makes all the difference.

BS 3 - *Those that can't do, teach.*

Man, oh man.

This was a biggie.

You see my second idea, the one I had been ignoring for so damn long, was to start to teach other bloggers and online publishers how to run their blogs like a business.

How to take this lovely creative thing they did already so naturally, and add a bit of business structure, strategy and systems to it.

There were already lots of courses out there about how to start a "hobby" blog.

But none about how to run one like a business (especially none actually taught by someone who had really done it!).

I wanted to show them how to do the things I had done right (only about 3% of blogs ever make enough money to even cover costs, so the fact that I had become a full-time blogger in under 12-months, and then ended up with a 5-person team made my business a bit of a unicorn in the blogging world).

And also how to avoid the things that I now know I did wrong (ah hindsight, you are a beautiful thing).

However I had this story in my head that not only was "teaching" a cop-out, taking the previously mentioned "easy" and therefore less worthy road.

It also meant you had failed.

It was the fall-back path, the safety net of the unsuccessful.

Add on top of that the bonus story of "Who was I to teach people anything when I had built my own business a bit broken anyway?"

So not only would I be taking the easy road, and then also admitting defeat in the process. I would be doing it disingenuously, and that was even worse.

Now can see why I was avoiding this whole idea for so long?

But as I was lying on the table that day I kept having all these flashes of conversations I had had with other bloggers and small business owners over the last few years.

Peers and people I admired.

Who, when we got down to talking business as we always seem to do, would actually take notes when I shared a strategy or idea, or just something that seemed pretty "common sense" to me.

They took notes!

And many of them also reported back later on about how that one simple thing I suggested to them had helped them and their businesses.

So surely if established and already successful people can find my advice useful, maybe less established ones will too?

Yes, this is what I think about when I am getting a massage (no wonder I don't do them that often!).

So I walked out of the Day Spa that day, headed home and wrote a quick blog post announcing an online course I was soon to be launching called Secret Bloggers' Business, teaching people everything I knew about running a blog like a business.

It was about 600 words, a stock photo and a simple PayPal button.

I published it the following day, included it in our weekly email and by the end of the week I had almost 100 people registered, and a whole new business off to an amazing start.

Making Friends with Money

Now once again I could finish this story here.

I could leave you with the Hollywood ending, the classic "hero's journey" from the bottom to the top via a couple of character building anecdotes along the way.

But once again that wouldn't be the whole truth.

Because you see there was still one very big lesson I needed to learn.

And it is the thing that really made a difference to my own financial success, and independence.

So, before we dig in I have to make a confession.

Up until quite recently my business had about $20,000 in credit card debt.

I was running two businesses that were turning over more than half a million dollars annually combined. I was paying myself a proper CEOs salary. But I still could just never seem to get around to being able to pay that debt down.

This was a debt that I had carried with me pretty much since starting my business. I would swap it from card to card (so I never really paid any interest on it), but for some reason, even when I managed to almost pay it down, something else would always come up (like a conference, or a needing a new computer), and like magic I'd be back at square one.

And this was my biggest lesson (and it's one that I am still working on to this day).

While I had always been good at *making* money.

And I had eventually figured out how to make money much more easily, and while still doing the things I loved.

I was never very good at knowing what to actually do with it when you had it.

I was awesome at spending it. Sure.

But I didn't know how to manage, or grow money.

The more you make, the more you spend. And as long as it all goes towards growing your business you're doing the right thing. Right?

And I am not talking about buy fancy shoes or cars here (I drive a Kia), but about hiring more people, investing in training, coaching, conferences and marketing, etc. (all good stuff, but where does it end?).

So once again I felt like it didn't really matter how much I earned, I only ever made "just enough".

And again, it turns out that knowing how to manage and grow your money is just not something people are taught.

We should be though, I think it should actually be a compulsory subject in school (imagine how many problems could be avoided if people, not just wealthy people with good advisers, knew this stuff?!).

I always thought this whole "money stuff" was the domain of stuffy-old, suit-wearing business people, not 30-something trainer-clad entrepreneurs.

And once again I found myself constantly just "one launch away" from finally cresting that new (and much bigger) wave.

So, how did I nip this cycle in the bud once and for all?

Well to be honest (that's what I do), it's still a work in progress, but I did do a couple of things that really helped.

First of all, I got reading. And one of the book's that really helped make all this "money stuff" much more understandable and real for me was a book called *Profit First* by Mike Michalowicz.

I won't go into WHAT he talks about, but I think it should be compulsory reading for all small business owners.

It's just a simple, common sense system for managing your money. But it works!

Secondly, I upgraded my bookkeeper, accountant and reporting software (because guess what, it's really hard to manage your money when you are not being told accurately how much of it you have and how much you are spending!).

And thirdly, once I had my head around how much I made, and had a clear budget for how much I could spend on my team, training and systems – I spent over a month overhauling pretty much every system, job role, program and schedule involved in running my business.

I had to get super clear on where I wanted the business to go, and how and who was going to get us there.

Not the most fun process in the world, and not one you can do without hard data and your ducks all in a row. But now I am out the other side of it, I feel like a hundred-pound weight has lifted and for the first time ever I feel a real sense of "ease" when it comes to making money and running my business.

Oh, and I did one more thing.

I closed down my first business.

Yep, after nearly nine-years of slog and soul, I had to let her go.

I looked into selling her (yes, my business was a definitely a female!), but when it came to the crunch just couldn't bear it.

And while actually making that decision was one of the hardest things I have ever had to do (again, so much ego wrapped up in this business, and so much internal BS too). One of the really important life lessons everyone needs to learn is when to just let things go.

My first business taught me so much, and was my launch-pad into my second. And now that I have let it go, it's also opened up the space and opportunities for business number three, too!

Running a business is one of the best methods of personal growth around. And if you are lucky (and open to it), you'll fail-fast and learn your lessons quickly and that business (or the one that comes after it) will help you to grow yourself and your wealth in an immeasurably satisfying way.

Derek Doepker

Derek Doepker is committed to enlightenment, empowerment, and compassion. He is a coach, certified NLP practitioner, and author of over 6 bestselling books in personal development, self help, fitness, and authorship. His titles include <u>Break Through Your BS</u>, <u>Why You're Stuck</u>, and <u>Why Authors Fail</u>.

Growing up, he ate fast food every night, hated exercise, and was dead broke. After deciding he was meant for something greater, he went on a search to figure out how to change his life. He discovered the problem wasn't him, but rather his thinking and strategies that kept him stuck. Using the tips he picked up from studying psychology, he got in the best shape of his life, started his own business, and broke through many of the limiting beliefs that had kept him stuck for years.

He started writing originally on his blog http://excuseproof.com to share the insights he discovered after spending ten years studying the world's top experts in psychology, personal development, *health, fitness, and spirituality. Today he believes that transforming the world begins with transforming oneself through knowledge and understanding of our psychology.*

He shares practical tips for overcoming everyday challenges like limited time, limited budget, limited knowledge, or just plain lack of motivation. With the right strategies, anyone can develop more self discipline, self confidence, and self love.

To create better habits in 5 minutes a day, download a free audiobook edition of his Gold Medal Award Winning book <u>The Healthy Habit Revolution</u> by going to this website: excuseproof.com/healthyhabitaudiobook.

Download a free copy of his book <u>Why Authors Fail</u> by going to ebookbestsellersecrets.com/freebook.

Why Everything's So Easy for Me

"Everything seems so easy for you."

I cringe when I hear that. It often comes from friends and followers who see that I've published another bestselling book or launched a successful training course. What they don't know about are the years of struggle and failure I went through to build my foundation. What they don't see are the hundreds of hidden day-to-day mini-failures that eventually result in the seeming effortless success they witness. What they don't get is the key to effortlessness is relentless effort.

I don't cringe because I want them to think I have it hard. I cringe because I know they're setting themselves up for needless suffering. It's the same suffering I went through at the start of my journey in entrepreneurship. The suffering of constantly asking myself, "Why the hell is it so easy for *them*, and yet, even though I'm a smart guy who studies exactly what to do and follows through, it seems like pulling teeth for me to get even the slightest taste of success?"

In the early days I would hear the same old self-help platitudes like, "Thomas Edison failed 1,000 times before creating the light bulb." Whether that's the case or not, it's meant to instill the idea that failure is a stepping-stone to success. The problem is that didn't really make me feel a whole lot better when I was selling off my most prized music keyboard to pay the rent and sleeping on an air mattress for two and a half years at the start of my entrepreneurial journey.

There was something however that did make me feel better in the early days struggling to get any traction. It was telling myself, "This is all a part of my before and after story. Some day, I will share my story of struggle with others so they will be inspired. They will realize, if he can do it, I can do it too."

I'm grateful to say that became a reality. For the past three years, I've shared my story of going from a dead broke valet parker to multiple #1 bestselling self-help and fitness author. Now I look back at all my struggles with a sense of gratitude because no one really gives a shit about some dude that says, "Yeah, I decided to start a business and everything was really easy and now I'm financially independent."

Can you relate to wanting to inspire and help others? If so, realize it's the challenges you overcome that will create the connection to those you will serve. Author and speaker Greg Montanta (HeartVirtue.com) says, "Your pain is your credential."

When you take a deeper look here and realize a temporary setback is really a setup to serve others even more greatly, then you can get outside of your own ego and see failure as a price you pay to help others. Since many heart-centered entrepreneurs will do more for others than for themselves, doesn't it make it easier to endure challenges when you realize you're ultimately giving others the gift being inspired by your example of overcoming adversity?

I share this with you because on your journey to financial independence and beyond, you will experience what feels like setbacks and failures. It will likely hurt. There will be points where you'll feel like quitting.

I've found the only way to endure and break through these challenges is to be more committed to my cause than to my comfort. To come from a counter-intuitive place of not necessarily expecting success, but rather expecting failure and saying, "It's OK if I won't succeed. This is so important I must do it anyway."

By approaching something with such conviction you'd do it in spite of failure, you become unstoppable.

Now some may scoff and say, "Derek, that's ridiculous. You need to have a positive belief in yourself and tell yourself you will succeed!"

I'm all for positive affirmations. However I have a belief that success and failure are both illusions. They're all a mind game. If every setback I've ever experienced was really a setup for a breakthrough down the road, how can it really be called a set "back?"

Meet with Triumph and Disaster, and treat those two impostors just the same" – Rudyard Kipling

If you exercise a muscle with resistance training, does it get stronger?

No. It gets fatigued. It breaks down. It gets *weaker*… temporarily.

So why then does one exercise to get stronger? The temporary setback in strength isn't optional, it's *required* to breakthrough to greater strength. Weakness is the door one must enter for greater strength, and failure is the door one must enter for even greater success. Success and failure are two sides of the same coin.

So take any reference I make to success and failure with a greater perspective that these are simply terms thrown around with no meaning except the meaning you give to them. Treat them as equal partners, and any overwhelming joy or sadness about each one becomes neutralized allowing you to experience the greatest joy – the joy of experiencing whatever you get to experience right now in this moment on your never ending journey.

Yet let's not forget that for all of this intellectual philosophy that there is no such thing as failure, we're all still human. And as a human, I've experienced a lot of pain and what seems to be very real "failures" in my life. Often, the most tragically painful failures often involve other people who've failed me.

There's one kind of failure however that has a particularly unique sting to it, and that is the kind of failure only a creator experiences. This is the experience of pouring your heart and soul into a creation only to have it ignored, rejected, or worst of all completely ripped to shreds by a critic.

As a college student, I was getting my Bachelor's degree in music composition. While my expertise was in playing guitar, I decided to step outside of my comfort zone and take on orchestration. This means I would be composing music for a symphony orchestra to play. There was a contest held by my college that would reward the winning orchestral composition with a live performance of the piece by the school's orchestra. I have no idea why, but as soon as I heard about this competition a fire was lit inside of me and I *had* to win.

I suppose that was a bit unrealistic seeing as how I was completely outmatched. I was just some wannabe rockstar guitar player competing against composition students getting their Master's degrees. One thing I did have though was a big enough ego to believe I could, and would learn how to write the greatest piece of orchestral music the school of music had ever heard.

In addition to honing my skills with a private instructor during the fall semester, I ended up spending my entire Christmas break studying everything I could get my hands on about orchestration, analyzing classical and modern orchestral scores, and listening to endless hours of symphonic music.

When I returned to classes after break, the deadline to submit the piece was moved forward giving me less time than I anticipated. I now had about one week to finish my masterpiece that I had only barely started. So I did what any reasonable person would do that has a goal in mind – I went days without sleep, skipped classes, and simply did not leave my desk to stop working on my score until I had to go to the bathroom or eat. Never in my life have I worked so hard on something, although looking back it was less about working hard and more about being completely consumed in the work in the ultimate state of creative flow.

Somehow, I made the deadline and turned in what I believed to be the absolute greatest piece of music I had ever written. I smugly walked away imagining the judge's jaw dropping to the floor after he hears such a masterpiece. Now I just had to play the waiting game to see the results of the competition that I was pretty sure I had in the bag.

I ended up being right about one thing, I was able to beat the other people I was facing off against. I didn't however anticipate what would end up happening – they decided not to have any winner of the competition. They also offered reasons why my score, no matter how good it was, had its problems. Looking back they did have some good points, but I only remember rejecting everything that was said and adamantly defending my work as being more than good enough to deserve the once in a lifetime opportunity to hear it played by a live orchestra.

To have the greatest masterpiece you've ever created rejected can only be described as "soul-crushing." Especially in light of going days without sleep and pushing the physical limits of my body to create it. That's not counting the countless hours of study just to be able to pull off writing something like that in the first place with limited experience. Yet somehow despite all of the sadness, anger, and feeling of rejection, I still managed to walk away feeling proud of what I had accomplished. Little did I know this was only going to be the beginning of a series of failed creations.

The next area as a creator I ventured into was entrepreneurship. Entrepreneurs are known for having a thick-skin to withstand constant failure, so I was well prepared for the task. I've lost track of how many business projects I attempted while being a broke valet parker sleeping on an air mattress struggling to just get by, but I can certainly remember the big ones.

One project I was sure would change the world of fitness as we know it was to record about eighteen hours of audio training detailing ten years of personal research into diet, exercise, psychology, and supplementation. Then I would turn that into a 350 page book. This unique selling point was that this program would show people how to overcome any excuse they had like not enough time, money, or motivation.

After completing this, it was time to market it. Fortunately I had a plan. I had invested hundreds of hours into educating myself on marketing products including volunteering at seminars to get the inside edge of online marketing. While I knew I had a lot to learn, I figured being the smart guy I am it would all come together.

The first thing I needed was testimonials, so I offered it for sale to my family and friends at a name-your-own-price sale. This was a great idea to get a surge of initial sales, even if they were at a $1.

This idea, which to this day I think is genius, somehow managed to fail miserably after only a handful of people bought it. I realized I couldn't even *give away* my work to the people who supported me the most. While I had a lot of people congratulating me my accomplishment, somehow they missed the memo that it helps me more to actually buy the program than say "great job!"

Being open to feedback as to why this amazing product wasn't selling, I decided to ask marketers on a forum what they thought of my video sales letter for the product. They said my brand name sucked, my forced smile made me look like a serial killer, and no one wants to buy a product that focuses on long-term effort since people want a quick fix. Feeling those same feelings swell up inside of me just like when my music was rejected, I was completely disheartened. While I tried to remain open to what they were saying, I felt these people just didn't get it. So I continued on.

The book idea remained with me and eventually I discovered self-publishing through Amazon Kindle. Seeing this as a renewed opportunity to take my prior work and reach a new audience with it, I decided to test the waters by self-publishing a shorter version of my original 350 page fitness ebook. Just like before, it didn't sell.

In this case, I did what I usually do which is study everything I could on the topic. I released my second book, and for the first time I saw some sales to the tune of around a hundred dollars that month. Finally, I could cover the costs of my initial investment and have enough money left over to eat half a meal at a restaurant in Los Angeles. It was a small victory so long as I just ignored how many hundreds to thousands of hours and dollars I invested to get there.

As a few more months went by, I was reaching a breaking point. I had decided long ago I wasn't ever going to give up on my dreams. I was going to make it or die trying. However, my logical brain was running out of options. I knew there was a way, but I was failing at every turn and my successes weren't big enough to be a light at the end of the tunnel. Luckily, something inside me said don't give up on the self-publishing thing, and so I decided to publish a third book.

By this point, I had invested thousands of dollars and hours into studying marketing, fitness, and personal development over the past several years. Combining the learned knowledge with the experiential knowledge from all my prior failures, I decided I was going to create something that had elements from everything I had learned up to this point. Thanks to all of my prior failures, I had just enough of a "screw it" attitude to do something that just felt right and I didn't really care about what the outcome would be. I published the book and reached out to every contact I had to get support in promoting it.

Thanks to a magical combination of all my prior knowledge coming together, getting support from friends I had networked with over that last year, and a whole lot of luck based on the way Amazon promotes books, the book ended up becoming a #1 best seller within a week in one of the most competitive niches – weight loss. I made more money in one week than I had made in months of valet parking. I knew pretty quickly my life was never going to be the same – and it hasn't been.

Since that time, while I've had on-going failures and mistakes, I find success is far more consistent. The reason being is every single failure I had forced me to learn something which later helped me create success. The failures don't last, but the lessons I've taken away from them do. In that regard, I'm grateful for every failure I've had because it forced me, as a creator, to create not only better work, but create a lesson I can share to everyone who struggles with failure. *Nothing is really a setback if it's what you need to make your next breakthrough.*

Failure taught me to let go of my attachment to an outcome. It taught me to remain humble and teachable. It forced me to look for weak points to improve that would later be invaluable to my success.

One of the biggest ways failure helped me find success was to show me that doing the right things doesn't always lead to success. Sometimes you can do the right thing, work the hardest, and "be the best" and still fail miserably. This not only leads to humility, but I noticed it led to me letting go of my desire to control things. It taught me to let go of my feelings about how things "should be" and learn to embrace what is.

A quote by Jim Carrey that stands out to me "you can fail at something you don't want, so you might as well take a chance doing what you love." In the long run, I'm going to feel like a failure if I don't try. So I might as well try and fail but have no regrets.

I believe all fear of failure stems from a deeper root fear – the fear of loss. What if I lose a lot of time and money on this? What if I lose the approval of others? What if I miss out on something even better?

I've found there's one simple way to forever overcome the fear of loss.

Consider this…

How many people spend tens of thousands of dollars to get a college education for just a chance at a better job when they graduate? How many papers do they write they don't get paid for? How many interns are there doing unpaid work?

It seems totally natural in our society to put years and thousands of dollars into something in the name of education. So why then would it be any different with business?

Here's what I've found. When you value lessons more than successes, you'll never fear failure or loss again.

I look back in hindsight and realize that, because I didn't quit on my journey to financial independence, every dollar I've "lost" was returned 10x when I got the lesson from the experience. Loss, like failure, is an illusion.

While it certainly sucked to write hundreds of pages in books that didn't sell and feel like I wasted a few months of my life, it's almost laughable compared to how many papers I wrote in college that never made me a dime. When I think about thousands of dollars spend on training courses and experiments that didn't pan out, it's still a drop in the bucket compared to tuition costs for college for a degree that didn't result in any extra income.

When some people hear nine out of ten businesses fail, they either get too scared to start a business or try to create the perfect business the first time to be the exception.

A mentor of mine Brandon Broadwater takes a different perspective. So what if 9 out of 10 businesses fail? Just create ten businesses because the one that succeeds will pay you far more than a job would for the rest of your life and make up for the failed ones.

Obviously it's wise to learn from the mistakes of others and educate yourself to not fail needlessly. However I encourage you to remember that failure only exists if one fails to get the lesson from the experience. And any success that leads to complacency is really a failure to one's future self.

Instead, treat both success and failure as the imposters they are. Treat failure as simply feedback. And remember, wherever you're at is all a part of your before and after story.

Patrick King

Patrick King is a Social Interaction Specialist and Conversation Coach based in San Francisco, California. You can find more about Patrick and download free content and trainings at www.patrickkingconsulting.com

He is an internationally bestselling author - somewhere among the many clients throughout the years, he decided to flesh out his inner monologue and found that he had quite a bit to say.

He focuses on using his unique emotional intelligence and understanding of human interaction to break down emotional barriers, instill confidence, and equip people with the tools they need for success.

When he's not helping clients conquer the world, he's either fronting an 80's cover band or training for his next 10k.

The Humble Beginnings Are What Truly Matter

It's probably fair to say that I have a lot of titles at this point (end of 2016).

Social skills and conversation coach, Social Interaction Specialist, international bestselling author, teacher, consultant, course designer – the list goes on.

But the titles that are the most important are the ones that I don't mention anymore. Former dating coach, former corporate lawyer…oh yeah, and late bloomer.

The reason these are so much more important, especially in talking about my path, is because they represent huge deviations I've made to get to wherever you might consider me right now.

But that's the thing, without any of those intermediate stumbles or steps, I can assure you that I wouldn't be where I am right now. The path to any type of success, and indeed progress itself, is always windy, and the perfect opportunity will never come to you when you're looking for it.

Am I grateful for the massive amount of debt I incurred by going to law school? Well, no. But without that sunk cost, who knows where I would be?

So let's start at the beginning.

I started studying for the LSAT because I was about to graduate with a degree in clinical psychology. I had a fair interest in psychological research, and one of my favorite courses in college was neurobiology. But as I looked at the people I was working under in research labs, I just couldn't see my life playing out running social experiments on people or working years for a PhD in psychology just to attempt to become a professor.

Comparatively, law school sounded like a fairly good alternative. I had interned at a law office for a couple of summers, I knew that they had a high salary, and I suppose some might call it a prestigious position. I could live with those things!

I almost dropped out of law school in the middle of my first year because it was starting to feel like a terrible fit. Things I had prided myself on such as my interpersonal skills, personality, and sense of creativity were things that were expressly rejected by the law... and my grades reflected it.

Law, in fact, is about jamming everything in your path into strict confines dictated by thousands of cases over the years, which means that your role is essentially a high-priced hammer. That's why lawyers are seen as risk-averse – they're just acting within those strict confines.

I persevered for reasons such as sunk cost and thinking I wasn't seeing the jungle through the trees and ended up working for a criminal judge my first summer.

I thought it might be a good fit, so I started working for the local district attorney's office as a volunteer, and can safely say that I started to dread going into work by the third week.

That was the first direction I took – this is important to note, because I feel like what has separated me from many people is that

I have taken action where others might be seeking their most ideal and perfect choice. Maybe it's because I always view every option as a compromise of some sort, but regardless of the reason. I tend to act before I think. This has occasionally been detrimental, but has served me well in my road to freedom, especially because it's the simple act of *acting* that most people will never complete.

With the notion of criminal law squashed, I had to aim elsewhere with my budding law career. I was lucky enough to go to law school in San Francisco, where I still reside, and was surrounding by startups and technology companies.

This was a time where there was a veritable feeding frenzy when a company with any sort of revenue or business plan would instantly qualify for millions in venture funding. Most importantly, it was modern and exciting, so I was drawn to corporate and startup law.

I thought that even if the work itself wasn't thrilling, if I could work with companies and clients that were literally changing the world, I could feel a sense of belonging.

I think you can predict where this went – it just wasn't my cup of tea, and I soon realized that it was because I wanted to be tossing around business ideas with the company rather than drafting their corporate stock plan.

I must have unconsciously known this to some degree because I had already started exploring other industries and positions while I was still a full-time practicing lawyer.

I always had a keen interest in human interaction and dating – it was what I would always talk about in my free time, with friends and even strangers. I just liked hearing about these situations and dissecting them to understand the *why*. *Tell me about your date and what did he text you afterwards* was always more compelling to me than asking about someone's work matters.

This manifested in two ways, initially.

First, I wrote online dating profiles for roughly 15 of my friends who, in very San Francisco fashion, were complaining about being single yet doing nothing about it. When you do anything that many times, you develop a systemized approach to doing things, and I had conveniently learned about Amazon's self-publishing program at the time, so it felt natural to memorialize my approach in my first book, which was entitled "Did She Reply Yet? The Gentleman's Guide to Owning Online Dating."

I had no intentions of making money with the book, but it started selling by nothing other than luck, and I quickly put up an accompanying website offering my services as an online dating coach.

The second way my personal interests manifested in my life was that, since I had gained a small amount of renown among my immediate circle for my book and online dating profiles, I was introduced to a mutual friend who ran a matchmaking company. Thus, I became a matchmaker for some of Silicon Valley's richest and brightest for a short period of time.

Do these two manifestations allow you to predict where I am right now? Only in hindsight.

But that's an important distinction I want to harp on repeatedly. If there's anything anyone can learn from my journey, it's that you have to *start* your journey.

You need to do something about it. Where you start won't be where you end up, it's just a stepping stone. That's the best way to view it – it's a stepping stone and it's fine for the time being while you figure out what works and doesn't work for you. Only then can you make some sort of educated decision.

It's only through the journey that you will find where you actually want to be, versus what you think *sounds nice*. There are always a million reasons to not start a journey to start working on an interest or business venture, but it's up to you to realize that (1) it's probably rooted in the fear of failure, or (2) you have incredibly unrealistic and high expectations about your path.

For example, my interest was in dating and human relationships, so I started doing this for my friends, put a website up, sent out guest blogs, networked with people in the space, and wrote for fun. It was only through this actual application that I could see which parts of the process, niche, and work I actually enjoyed, and it was only through this application that opportunities within the parts that I liked would become visible to me.

My path was a complete series of "I might as wells" that lead to "This sounds like a good opportunity – but the latter would never come if I hadn't trudged through the former. Too many people I meet want to start their journey with their perfect unicorn idea, not knowing what they don't know about the industry and space.

Mind you, I was also doing all of this with the "safety net" of my law job – I was doing this all in my free time because I simply enjoyed it. Talking to people about who they want to date, and writing dating profiles for people? That's stuff that I truly would have done for free, in my free time. So in that sense, I was lucky to be able to take an interest of mine and make money with it even if that wasn't my intention to start with. Really, mark a victory for simple dumb luck and timing, and putting myself out there when I saw some results.

The reason I wanted to start talking about my journey from way back in the beginning was because I wanted to show how much I had invested into my law career. Including studying for the LSAT, that was a good six years of my life. I had a good position and promising career trajectory, from a purely professional sense. Most would consider me as someone with a lot to lose.

And yet, at some point, what does it matter? I believe that the people who will actually take action are those that hit a critical mass of discontent. That's the common thread I see with people similar to me – they feel there is no other choice but to diverge from the path they were set on.

Me, I couldn't see myself living my life in my cubicle, filling out paperwork at a desk that seemed more confining with each passing day.

We all have friends who complain day in and day out and never do anything because their sense of discontent is minor compared to (1) their fear of failure and lack of belief in themselves, (2) their aversion to hard work, and (3) their fear of losing security. That's not to say that there is a right or wrong – but this is why some people will talk the talk and complain your ears off yet never take action. If you hit that critical mass of discontent, none of those factors matter.

At this point, I was starting to see an income that, while nowhere near a corporate lawyer salary, was more than just a side hustle income. To me, that was a sign that I knew enough to be able to scale everything and continue growing. I also reasoned that since I had only been doing this on the side for less than a year, that I could immerse myself in the niche and truly learn what else I could do.

While I was fairly insulated from feelings of self-doubt and failure because I was just taking action, on the side, on an interest/passion of mine, without a clear intent to make it a full time career, these feelings started to come up once I told people what I did on my time off and my plans of leaving the law. This was a big step for me because the vast majority of my friends were professionals – lawyers and doctors and the like.

They just couldn't comprehend that I wanted to *make money online*, and thought that I was insane for leaving the law. It was something that was so foreign to them – and I'm in San Francisco! This is a town where there are no fewer than seven food delivery companies, so you can imagine the reaction of people in a less tech-centric city.

As you might expect, my parents were right at the forefront of doubt and skepticism. They weren't so much disturbed by the foreign-ness of the notion, they instead were rightfully concerned by the stability and security of such a job (as if law firms are stable and care about you...). That was an interesting dichotomy of reactions, and directly showed the priorities of the people in my life – my parents just wanted to make sure that I would be okay, while my friends were mostly curious about hanging out with someone unconventional.

As my business started showing growth every month, my parents became my biggest cheerleaders, while my friends' reactions ranged mostly from confusion to amusement, likely assuming that I was just barely scraping by. It was the darndest thing.

I began searching for people to look up to and emulate.

This wasn't a conventional path I was setting out on, and there were no tried and true paths I could generally follow.

I found a few people touting their success, but this would prove a challenge in itself because the only people you'll find that tout themselves as Internet entrepreneur role models are the exact people that you don't want to follow. You know the type I'm talking about.

I quickly got seduced by Instagram accounts that promised constant travel, working on laptops adjacent to beaches, and unlimited mai tais without a single thought as to whether that sort of nomadic and untethered life was a good fit for me.

This was probably the biggest hurdle for me, and one I struggle with to this very day. Now that I have the exact freedom that most people can only dream about – what is the optimal lifestyle for me? It's almost a case of too much freedom that causes analysis paralysis.

So as many in my position do, off I went to Southeast Asia for economic arbitrage and a relaxed lifestyle… then off to South America and Europe for about 5 months total until I realized that those Instagram accounts do not represent the lifestyle I want, despite having the freedom to do it. It's like seeing a picture of a gourmet meal and craving that meal, only to find that the meal contains ingredients that you are allergic to. You just never know what you want until you actually experience it.

People will sell you on their lifestyles, morning routines, and schedules, but in the end, they aren't you. Make sure that your road to financial freedom represents a lifestyle that you want. In other words, know your "WHY" for doing it all, and then double down on that. Don't let other people tell you what your "WHY" is. Just because you have a degree of freedom doesn't mean that you're happy utilizing it, even.

What's interesting about the Internet space is that no one really has all the answers like they do in the law.

That might be the only thing I miss about working as a lawyer – there was almost always a right or wrong answer, regardless if the opposition wanted to acknowledge it. We all read the same laws and cases, so there was a very conventional way of doing things that almost never failed.

The Internet business space is full of hucksters that will tell you that they have the answers, but in reality, they might just know a modicum more than you to make you think they know the world. And then they'll charge you for their knowledge, which they only acquired to be able to sell people on – not through experience or their own struggles and learning.

So anytime you want to learn something new, put something into application, or even create something, you need to do probably three times as much research as any other space simply because whoever you're reading – it just might experience as an outlier, or they are leaving out vital parts of the puzzle that would give you success. You need to check, double check, and then get two more dissenting opinions before ultimately making your own decision without a "conventional way" to fall back on. It's hard, hard work.

Because of that, networking is an essential currency for being an entrepreneur. Just having someone to guide you through something for the first time, or offer a helpful pointer here or there because something has worked better for them, can make all the difference over a series of months or years. It's a hugely cumulative effect.

The nature of my work – coaching, creating, and writing – is extremely solitary, so networking and meeting like-minded people also serves the purpose of keeping me sane. After all, you talk about work with your friends. If your friends have no concept of what you do and aren't interested, you have to have an outlet for that somewhere. Some of these "Internet friends" I talk to far more than my "real life friends" simply because the Internet is our daily water cooler, so to speak. I make every effort to guide and give advice to people who reach out to me because I still remember those who never bothered to return my emails when I was just starting out.

I'm also far more willing than I ever thought possible to pay for information to save my time. Courses, coaching, and outsourcing, for example, are things I routinely engage in, because that's simply the shortcut for me to get to where I need to be. If these options weren't available for me, I would have to spend countless hours researching, guessing at which path is correct, and ultimately not producing what I need to for my business.

This leads to me another hurdle that I and many others constantly deal with – the value of time. I can say it now – I value my time very highly…

Yet since I value my time more, it's like I'm putting a dollar sign on every minute or leisure time as an opportunity cost to work more, because in my business, if I'm not working, no money is coming through the door. There's a fairly direct correlation.

There's something to be said for a work-life balance where you can turn your brain off 100% when you're not at your laptop. Unfortunately, I'm not close to that point yet, and have trouble keeping my weekly working hours below 60.

Overall, my path to where I am now has been relatively breakdown-free and quick.

I do think I played a part in this. I built my personal brand while I was still a practicing lawyer, and I enjoyed the learning process because I loved the field. At some point, I figured out how to monetize my knowledge in the field, and then I worked at the skills to get good at the monetizing aspects.

I jumped in headfirst and made it my goal to simply explore and pursue the opportunities that were in front of me at the moment. I didn't want to run before I could walk, and maybe this delayed gratification served me well as I surveyed the entire field of human interactions and was able to find my own spot in it.

But I'd be either supremely arrogant or a fool to not admit that luck laid all of these opportunities to me at the right time in my life, and that I happen to excel at most of the skills required for my new line of work.

My final recommendation to those seeking to create their own path to freedom: passion is not enough. In fact, passion is very little. The preferred P for me is proficiency. Finding my spot in my field was simply a matter of finding where my proficiency lay.

For that reason, one of the books I most identify with in my winding path is So Good They Can't Ignore You by Cal Newport. I believe it's a tremendously important book, especially for someone that wants to make a change in their life.

Newport asserts that people start to feel passionate about what they feel good at, and once they have a certain level of proficiency, they can use that proficiency to take control, make an impact, and fulfill their bigger purposes. Focus on attaining a level of proficiency in things, and then seek to capitalize on them – otherwise, what are you doing that people will care about? What are you doing that people would pay you for, and how are you spending your time?

It's the only way people will pay you money to do things.

Dilbert creator Scott Adams says it better than I ever will:

"The first thing you should learn in a course on entrepreneurship is how to make yourself valuable. It's unlikely that any average student can develop a world-class skill in one particular area. But it's easy to learn how to do several different things fairly well. I succeeded as a cartoonist with negligible art talent, some basic writing skills, and an ordinary sense of humor and a bit of experience in the business world. The "Dilbert" comic is a combination of all four skills. The world has plenty of better artists, smarter writers, funnier humorists and more experienced business people. The rare part is that each of those modest skills is collected in one person. That's how value is created."

Everything else flows from the value you create.

Andi Cumbo-Floyd

Andi Cumbo is a writer, an editor, and a writing coach, who lives at the edge of Virginia's Blue Ridge Mountains with her husband, 4 dogs, 4 cats, 6 goats, and 28 chickens. She writes regularly about writing and the writing life at Andilit.com, and her books include The Slaves Have Names, Writing Day In and Day Out, Steele Secrets, and Discover Your Writing Self. She also still regularly crochets stuffed animals, but she doesn't need to sell a giraffe to buy groceries anymore.

From Professor to Portable Toilets to Farm-Life Bliss: My Winding Road to the Life I Dreamed

In 2009, I quit my full-time position as an English professor, a position I had worked for over 10 years to achieve. I left because, in short, I was burnt-out, overworked, and not writing. The choice to leave was hard because I love teaching, because I had no steady work prospects, and because I adored my colleagues, but I had no doubts about leaving. It was absolutely the right thing to do for my health and for my writing.

For the next year and a half, I pieced together income by reversing the path I had taken into teaching. I returned to adjunct work and online tutoring. Even then, the fact that I had really taken three steps back in the hopes of, maybe, somehow, taking four steps forward wasn't lost on me. I had retreated to the familiar territory of hours in the car between schools, evenings on my computer to help people who often plagiarized their work, and no medical insurance. Surely, this wasn't what I was intended to do for the rest of my life.

Still, I had no regrets. Really. I did, however, eat a lot of Chik-Fil-A in the car.

Then one day, I got a call from my dad when I was in office hours. "It's gallbladder cancer," he said. "We'll find out your mom's treatment soon." I stood there on the lawn of this gorgeous liberal arts college and breathed the September air. September 18th. I don't know why I remember that date.

A few weeks later, I was on my way to teach a class when my mom said the words "palliative care." I almost drove head-on into northern Virginia commuter traffic. She was dying.

By my birthday in early November, she had been hospitalized, and I had gone down to be with her. A week later, I got coverage for my classes at one school, managed to set out a plan to teach the final weeks of the other via Skype, and went home to central Virginia to be with my mom as she died. She left us on Thanksgiving Day 2010.

I must have submitted final grades during the week after her death, but I have no idea how. I don't remember much of that holiday season at all.

When Christmas came, I was deep in grief, jobless, and unclear about my next steps, but I knew I couldn't teach now. Teaching required too much of me, at least in the way I taught. I didn't hold myself back in the classroom; I gave myself to the connection with my students. And a teacher who couldn't stop crying or disappeared into grief-induced moments of reflection wasn't effective. So I told the schools I wouldn't be back, and my dad, brother, and I went and moved my things from northern Virginia the week after Christmas.

My three cats, 60 boxes of books, and I moved back home to figure out what was next.

A couple of weeks later, Dad and I were on a return trip from visiting my grandmother in NC. It had mostly been a quiet ride, our attention tuned to *The Story of Edgar Sawtelle*, which played through the car's speakers.

Then, at a stop light in Goldsboro, Dad asked what I wanted to do. "I want to teach at a liberal arts college, full-time." My mind still believed that college teaching was my calling and that if I could just get a lower-intensity position – I had been teaching a 5-course-per-semester load at a community college before – I would be able to write and teach.
"What do you need to do that?" Dad asked.

"A book. I need to publish a book."

"Live with me. I'll pay your bills for a year. Write your book."

That is how 18 months in my childhood home came to me. That is also how my first book, *The Slaves Have Names*, began. At a stoplight, with a father and daughter in grief and unknowing together.

For the next year and a half, I researched and wrote a book about the people who were enslaved on the plantation where my dad lived and had worked for over twenty years as the farm and tree-nursery manager. I used the gift of time that my dad gave me, and I gave myself to the people in those pages. When I was done, I had 22 profiles of those strong, perseverant individuals interwoven with my personal journey of coming to know them. It was a good book.

I should pause here and say that my father is, hands-down, the most generous person I know. He gave me $1,000 a month during that year and a half, and he asked only that I do my work and be a good roommate. (I think I was except for the possum that I accidentally let in one night, but that's another story.) He bought the groceries. He didn't ask where his money went (student loans, research expenses, haircuts, and time with friends, mostly). He watched the first season of *The Voice* with me and enjoyed it.

Then, one day, he said, "Your mother and I saved all this money to travel, and now, well, now I have no one to travel with. I want to use that money, instead, to help you and your brother with your dreams."

That, then, was the way my dad came to buy me a farm, a place I had dreamed of owning for many years.

God's Whisper Farm, as I named it, was a small, blue house of 757-square-feet that sat on a sloping 10 acres at the edge of Virginia's Blue Ridge Mountains. The house had been empty for a couple of years, and so it was infested with stink bugs and reeked of cat urine. Still, the moment I saw it, I knew it was home. So Dad bought it. No mortgage. No obligation to me. Just the first, smelly steps toward my dream.

He and I worked on that farm. We cleaned, repaired, and did small remodels to the house. He hired his crew from the tree nursery to come over and clean the landscape. One of the men pushed a walk-behind bush hog into grass so tall I quickly lost sight of him. We cleared dead fall and pushed logs into a burn pile that turned into one of the largest, controlled (mostly) bonfires I've ever seen.

Within 6 weeks, it was ready, and I moved into the home of my dreams.

Now, though, I had to make my own money. Dad would have helped still if I'd asked, and he did pay for all the work on the house. But I knew I needed to get my feet under myself financially then.

I had been teaching a few online courses of my own design, short, six-week modules on creative nonfiction, poetry, short story. My former colleagues had also continued to give me online courses in professional writing to teach. Plus, I'd picked up a little editing work for a nonprofit. But that wasn't enough income to cover my expenses – even with a very small house and no mortgage.

Here, then, I began to get a little nervous. I was living on less than $1,000 a month, and with almost a quarter of that required for my student loans, I wasn't exactly flush.

Still, generosity saved the day. Friends of my blog, Andilit.com, which I had been writing since February 2007, sent me mixing bowls and cash to help. Other friends bought the crocheted stuffed animals I was making for my Etsy shop. Still others came by the farm and helped me clean up the trash that had been left all over the would-be pasture.

I made it through, but it was tough. I didn't eat much, and my puppy Meander and I did our best to use the heat and hot water as little as possible. I didn't have a TV and data for the internet was limited, so I read a lot and cuddled under blankets with the dog at night to watch my luxury of one hour of *The Vampire Diaries* every evening.

I was happy.

Then, happiness went up a notch when a guy I met online showed up at my house for our first date with bags of groceries. We'd talked a lot, and he'd read most of the archives on my blog. He knew I was in dire financial straits, so when he unloaded cheese and eggs and yogurt, stocked the fridge with Dr. Pepper and bread, I was already falling a little bit.

Not long after, he bought me my own chainsaw and came to spend days working to clean up the trails on the farm with me (spoiler: we got married less than a year later.).

Friends were also generous with work referrals. My friend Casey told me that her brother was looking for someone to help with his web design and SEO company, so I Googled the definition of SEO and went to work as a project and social media manager for his company. I wrote Facebook and Twitter updates for a portable toilet company and drafted copy for our own website. I learned about domain names and how to really use Google Analytics. I was in the know about Facebook insights when they first came out, and my colleague Aaron taught me how to check a website's functionality and discoverability.

Then, one of that company's employees broke off to start her own virtual assistant business and hired me as a freelancer to help with writing copy for her client's websites. I now had regular, if not plentiful, income, and all that I was learning from these jobs I was able to apply to my own website.

Soon, other friends were sending me referrals for editing, and I landed my first real client – an erotica novelist who had just secured a 12-book contract. (I was a bit jealous.) Between the work I did for her, the editing jobs I was able to secure through an online job site, and freelancing for the website and VA companies, I was working pretty steadily now.

Those were still hard days. I spent most of December 2012 frantically crocheting stuffed animals for 14 hours a day since the holiday slump had left me without much editing or website work. I was still barely making more than $12,000 a year, and I wasn't loving the work I was doing for the website companies, mostly because of poor management.

Still, I needed to do what I needed to do, especially since I now had a farm to grow. So I kept on, keeping on.

By the spring of 2013, I had edited 10 books, mostly through personal referrals, and I was able to step back from the online referral site and save myself the frustration of being told over and over again that my very reasonable rates ($15 an hour) were too expensive. Now, word-of-mouth was starting to grow my business.

I had also published my first book after taking the advice of my friend Laraine Herring who suggested, when I finished the edits of *The Slaves Have Names*, that I write the next thing. So I wrote *God's Whisper Manifesto: The Makings of a Dream* in the first months on the farm. A friend designed the cover for free, and another friend bartered with me – editing for formatting. It was a small book, something that articulated the principles by which I wanted to live on the farm. It didn't sell many copies, but it did catch some attention. A few months after it was published, a woman I had met online told me the book had really inspired her, and she offered to put together a book re-launch for me. She also told me to raise the price. Between our efforts, we sold a few more copies. The financial stress eased a bit more.

I also got chickens that next spring, and so I saved $6 a month on eggs.

By May 2013, Philip and I were planning a wedding, a wedding that we needed to pay for.

He worked full-time, and so his salary was going to be our core income. But the cost of a wedding was high. Still, we did as much of it as we could ourselves – we grew the potatoes and green beans for the meal, and we made the signage and borrowed some of the decorations. A local cut-flower farm gave us a great deal on some of the most beautiful flowers I've ever seen, and on September 28, 2013, we wed. Our friends gave us gifts of cash to use on our honeymoon, and we spent a beautiful week in Maine together.

When Philip and I married, things did get easier. The stability that came with our combined lives made it possible for me to sever ties with one employer when I was put in a position of overseeing too many projects without enough experience.

Too, I was finally able to get that book out into the world. I had been shopping *The Slaves Have Names* around to agents for a year, and I'd gotten some interest but no one willing to commit to the book.

I could have kept shopping it, but I'm an impatient person, and I was hoping it would help us pay some bills. So I self-published the book in November 2013, just a few weeks after our wedding. Philip and I designed the cover, and I formatted the print book myself. (I also then vowed never to do that again. It was infuriating, and I never did get the headers right.) A friend bartered with me for the eBook formatting, and out my first print book came, her cover a little pixellated but her content rich and good.

The book did really well. Friends in the African American history and genealogy communities latched onto it, and my hometown historical society held a big event for the release as did the library. Two friends who owned businesses in my hometown sold copies on their counters, and they sold more copies than anyone, even

Amazon. Friends online scheduled a book tour for me through Ohio, where I spoke at genealogy groups and homeschool coops. And online sales were strong, too. I was pleased.

Now, I had something about which to speak and something to sell when I spoke. A turning point for sure.

But not back to teaching. Even with the book in hand, it was clear that teaching was not going to be my path any longer. I can't really articulate why that was. But I knew I needed to be at home, to be working with words as much as possible. So I stayed with my freelancing gigs and committed even more fully to my personal business.

Eventually, in December 2014, I quit the website company job because of poor management that had plagued the business, and I then hired my colleague from that business, Aaron, to redesign Andilit.com. It was the first time I was able to hire a designer for my site, and that small investment brought big returns for my business. That was a lesson I would continue to learn – pay a little now to get more later.

One of the perks of freelance editing for entrepreneurs is that you get to read all their content without having to pay for any of it, and in that role, I came across some great entrepreneurial advice about recurring income. It made perfect sense – if I could get people to pay me on a monthly basis for something, I could have some freedom to not always have to be digging up clients. So in August 2014, I launched the Painted Steps Writer's Program, named after the stairs in our farmhouse that Philip had painted like the spines of our favorite books.

Painted Steps was a six-month, group-coaching program that guided people through the process of drafting their first book. It was comprised of weekly group video chats, weekly emails of encouragement and guidance, bi-weekly individualized phone calls with me, and monthly feedback on a set of written pages, all for just $150 a month.

I had four people enroll in the first session, and it was great. I had steady income, and they had accountability and community for their writing. (By the way, that first group still meets on a monthly basis to talk about writing and share their work.)

I only ran one additional session of Painted Steps, and it was successful, too, but not in the way I had hoped. It took more time and energy than I had available, and it didn't seem to get people as far along as I'd hoped it would. I may go back to that model sometime, but for now, it's a tabled. Not a failed experiment but a less than ideal one.

About that same time, I held my first writer's retreat at the farm. 13 people spent a weekend camping on the grounds (or staying in a local B&B if they preferred), and we did an open mic reading, enjoyed a Saturday night concert, had craft talks, and participated in group workshops on the mountainside. As a financial endeavor, it was a bust – we had not anticipated the amount of beer and wine a group of writers can go through in three days. But as a business beginning, it was one of the smartest things I did.

In July of 2016, we held our third retreat with over 20 writers, and this time, I partnered with Shawn Smucker and Kelly Chripczuk, two friends and fellow writers, to organize, promote, and plan the event. I also asked my mother-in-law and step-mother to cook for us, and that was a huge success in terms of both eating and energy.

We hired guest speakers to talk about various craft and publishing topics, and we each made a few hundred dollars, which is a success since we're all small business owners who are still in the growth phase. Our plans for 2017 include a slightly larger group and a slightly higher cost.

Over the next two years, I continued to build my editing business largely, as has always been the case for me, through the generous referrals of friends including the wonderful publishing expert Jane Friedman. I am now booking clients at least two months out, and I get queries about my editing and manuscript review services almost every day. It's quite a different scene from when I was paying to bid on editing opportunities through that referral service.

I also have a regular coaching clientele that is growing every week. Some of these folks came to me through Painted Steps, some through my books and website, and some through a free course I offered this year as a lead magnet for my list. That course, Discover Your Writing Self, had over 900 people enrolled in it, and it was the single-most effective list-building tool I've used yet.

I regularly speak both about slavery and about writing. This afternoon, in fact, I am speaking to a writer's group that is made up of retired women who are eager to know what to do when they are done with the drafts of their books.

In the past year, I have published two books myself, keeping to the self-publishing model I know and that has better financial returns than traditional publishing: *Steele Secrets*, a young adult novel about a girl who helps to save an abandoned slave cemetery after she sees the ghost of an enslaved man, and the book version of the *Discover Your Writing Self* course. In November 2016, the sequel to *Steele Secrets, Charlotte and the Twelve* will be out, so I'll be up to three books a year, a pace I hope to continue. My book sales don't yet make me the kind of income I'd like them to bring in, but with each new book, I learn more about how to make it enticing and about how to promote it. Plus, the more financial freedom I have from my editing and coaching business, the more able I am to devote resources to design and promotion. Then, when I sell more books, I can write more books. It's a beautiful cycle.

In 2015, I cleared over $60,000 from my writing business, which is not comparable to the sales figures of the great entrepreneurs like Pat Flynn or Amy Porterfield, whose podcasts help me grow my business in great ways. But for someone like me, who is dedicated to art, who isn't interested in hiring employees or scaling up to big heights with products, I feel good about what I do. I am sincere in my work, personalized in my approach, and dedicated to working with writers, particularly first-time writers, who need a gentle kick in the tush from time to time.

My income combined with my husband's salary has meant that we could move to a slightly-larger farm that is much closer to his job. We now have goats, and our chicken flock has grown. We built a barn in which we hold our writers' retreats and regular concerts, readings, and craft shows, with some financial assistance from my dad again. (Told you he was generous.) My dog Meander now has a companion, a basset hound named Mosey, and we're talking about adding some buck goats to our herd to begin breeding this fall. Angora rabbits will be joining the crew soon, too.

I now live the life I have always dreamed of but never imagined possible. I spend my days and nights in a place that feeds my soul, with animals who give me joy and may, one day, earn their keep, too. (Meander did have her own calendar for sale one year.) I do the work I love all day every day.

I spend my days helping writers live their dreams even as I feed my own soul. I owe all of this to the generosity of people who love me and appreciate my work. From my father's farm gift to Philip's bags of groceries to the countless referrals to the mixing bowls that I make regular omelettes in, it's generosity that has made all of this possible, and I work every day to return that kindness with my work. My business would not exist with the kindness of others, and I will never forget that.

Bryan Cohen

Bryan Cohen is an actor, freelance writer, author and an occasional game show contestant. He has written over 30 books, which have sold more than 30,000 copies. His newest book is <u>Ted Saves the World</u>, the first book in a new YA paranormal/fantasy series.

Bryan lives with his wife and their Netflix account in Chicago.

He loves writing weekly emails to his subscribers. Join that list at bryancohen.com/subscribe.

He's also been keeping a blog to help creative writers find new inspiration for the last five years. Check out Build Creative Writing Ideas here: www.build-creative-writing-ideas.com.

Presents, Passion, and Potholes

My Christmas week was pretty darn depressing. It was 2008, and I was answering phones for some company I didn't care about. Temping paid the bills (barely), but it left me feeling dispensable, interchangeable, and lonely. While my girlfriend was off with her family and my parents rang in the holidays thousands of miles away, I was waiting for the familiar noise of a receptionist ringtone. Most of the company's clients had stopped working days ago, making my job answering phones both easy and mind-numbingly boring.

But I had a plan. A plan to pass the hours. A plan that would eventually turn my life around…I was going to start a blog. And in the 35 work-free hours of my paid 40-hour workweek, I set up the building blocks of a career.

With an English and Drama degree in my back pocket, I always knew it was going to be difficult to ensure my skills would be applicable in the real world. The real challenge was simple and treacherous: how was I supposed to do creative work when it wasn't assigned by a teacher? In the three years after school, I'd mostly answered that question with a hearty, "I'll write when the inspiration strikes!" Unfortunately, much like cable TV customer support, inspiration isn't at all reliable.

I'm not sure what prompted me to take a week most people think of as a deserved break and turn it into a fevered writing sprint. Perhaps it was the fact that I was getting paid for my time regardless. Maybe, I wanted to look busy in case my supervisor walked by. I'd like to think I was inspired in part by the fact that I wasn't living the life I wanted. Whatever the reason, that week I laid the foundation for my career as an author and a thought leader. That week, I worked.

It would take some time to reap the benefits.

From Blogs to Books

Flash ahead to August 2010. I was still doing temp jobs from time to time, but I'd added freelance writing to my repertoire. Blogging for two years had given me the confidence to seek out additional writing gigs, but it had yet to pay for website hosting costs. Build Creative Writing Ideas was getting traffic. Through a research tool that came with my hosting package, I knew the keywords that were likely to get me the most searches and traffic. And they were working! The most successful keyword of the bunch was "creative writing prompts," a term for story starters that blocked writers use to get their juices flowing. As a trained improv comedian, writing ideas for scenes was a cinch, allowing me to come up with over 70 topics of prompts with about 10 on each page. Hundreds of random internet people visited my site every single day, and yet, I couldn't figure out how to get paid for my efforts. Ads almost helped me break even, but I could no longer afford to lose money anywhere in my life. I wondered if it was time to cut my losses and try out something else. Maybe my ex-employer Starbucks would re-hire me. At least I'd get free coffee, right?

I scoured the web for a financial option that wouldn't have me crawling back on my hands and knees to the green and white giant. I made a list of the most promising ideas, but one tactic shot to the top without question. It turned out; you could take your existing blog posts and collect them into a PDF that people would buy. In other words, I could write a book without having to start from scratch. For a guy who was too lazy to start a blog until he was being paid for his time by a temp agency, repurposing my content sounded like a great idea.

I counted up my prompts and found I was in the mid-700 range. I buckled down and wrote 30 more blog posts with 10 prompts each to get me up to an even 1,000. After creating the ugliest book cover ever observed by humankind, I posted the PDF on my website. My future mother-in-law bought the first copy. A few strangers here and there snatched up about a dozen more copies. With high expectations, I considered my efforts a failure, but I didn't realize my momentous achievement at that time. I sold a product. I created something that another person wanted to buy. And when you know how to create products, it's only a matter of time before you get better, smarter, and more prolific.

One month later, I learned that PDFs were so 2009, and that Amazon let you publish real-live book listings on its website. Without having any clue whatsoever, I re-formatted *1,000 Creative Writing Prompts*, paid my girlfriend a pittance to create a much prettier cover, and launched my first real ebook into the world.

My patience was severely tested during the first month of Amazon crickets. I thought this might be another rabbit hole I'd dug myself into. I wondered if I'd ever make back the fifty bucks I gave my girlfriend to create a cover nobody would ever see. Instead of giving up, I took action. I made sure almost every page on my website linked to the book. I started setting up guest posts on other blogs. I even sought out reviewers for my not-very-well-edited debut.

Two Christmases after my lonely temp week, I carried my laptop up to the guest bedroom in my future in-laws' house. Escaping the festivities for a few minutes here and there, I did exactly what I'd been doing every three hours or so for the previous 60 days. I checked my sales stats.

When the sales dashboard loaded, I readjusted my eyes. The first month of crickets had been followed by around 30 book sales in October. November had seen that number creep up to 50. I squinted again and called out for my girlfriend. When she arrived, I beamed with pride and told her the good news. My book had sold 20 copies THAT DAY!

At long last, I felt like I'd made it. If only I'd learned my lesson about what brought me that success in the first place…

Expanding My Catalogue, Contracting My Effort

The next three years truly proved the power of passive income. Through the magic of self-publishing on Amazon, I sold over 20,000 copies of my first book, pulling in 70% of every digital sale. With my increased income from the book and a cushy new freelance job, my girlfriend and I moved into a nicer apartment and life finally felt like it was moving in the right direction. I wrote several more books, though none were quite as successful as the first. Repurposing the prompts book into a series of workbooks started to bring in even more money and I began to kick back and relax. I coasted.

I wish that someone had told me that coasting was an entrepreneur's worst vice.

After two years of steady sales, my first book experienced a massive decline. Around the same time, my "easy money" freelance gig asked me to take a massive pay cut. A fortuitous and successful appearance on the game show "Who Wants To Be a Millionaire" helped to stem the financial bleeding and earned me enough to buy my girlfriend an engagement ring, but it wasn't enough to keep me afloat for long.

It's not like I didn't work between late 2010 and the beginning of 2014, but the biggest mistake I made was failure to learn and grow. I lucked into a successful debut book, but I never did the research to figure out what made it successful in the first place. I wrote thousands of blog posts for a high-paying freelance gig, but I failed to diversify my portfolio or come up with a backup plan. Readers were connecting with my work, but I failed to establish a deeper bond with them through an email list or a social media community.

I rested on my laurels and by the end of 2013, it was coming back to bite me.

Doing the Work

In 2014, I resolved to do the work and learn from my mistakes. I started listening to more podcasts to find out what was working for other authors. After hearing an episode of Simon Whistler's Rocking Self Publishing Podcast, I adapted an idea from horror author Timothy Long and created a Multi-Author Facebook Event. I used my skills of bringing people together from my theatre director days to gather a dozen nonfiction authors for a one-day self-publishing info extravaganza called "March to a Bestseller." Hundreds of authors came out to the event, which featured giveaways, a sale on books for authors, and some amazing discussions about publishing. The event helped forge friendships with some big names in the industry, which would later become valuable both from an information standpoint, as well as financially.

Getting that many authors together was definitely like herding cats. Making sure folks showed up and dropped the prices of their books for the sale was a complicated process. Most people wouldn't be willing to put up with that. Because I endured the stress of organizing the event, I was the one who earned the spoils.

One of those connections, Author Marketing Club's Jim Kukral, became the co-host of my first ever podcast: *The Sell More Books Show*. This weekly publishing news show helped me to learn more about publishing while establishing credentials as an authorpreneurial thought leader. The show was a bear to produce, requiring hours of hunting for the latest information so we were never out of date. It was (and still is) a ton of work, but I was willing to do what others wouldn't (or couldn't). The show has led to some incredible opportunities and more connections with influencers in entrepreneurship and self-publishing.

As I made more and more relationships with other authors, one friend helped me land a new and intriguing freelance job. The gig gave me the opportunity to ghostwrite articles for CEOs and influencers for major publications like Forbes, Entrepreneur, and Inc. The position was a major challenge and it stretched my skills as a copywriter. It didn't pay quite as well as my previous blogging job, but the lessons I learned from the position would pay major dividends going forward.

I continued to struggle financially in 2014 and through half of 2015. Some folks might have interpreted that as a sign to change up tactics. My instincts told me that even though my earnings had dropped and my debt was on the rise that I had to keep doing what

I was doing. I had a gut feeling that the connections I was making and the work I was doing was headed in the right direction. It's not always clear what the next step will be, but sometimes you just need to keep plugging away until you succeed. I'm glad I followed that instinct.

One piece of advice I picked up from my binges on learning was to form a mastermind group with smart folks in my field. While many teachings from the countless audiobooks and podcasts went in one ear and out the other, I actually followed up with this one. When a friend and fellow author invited me to a group, I joined and I committed to twice a month meetings for the foreseeable future. Masterminds are a fantastic way to get regular feedback on your ideas and whether or not you're making good choices. I told my fellow group members of my wins and losses and asked for recommendations on how to move forward in my business as an author and an entrepreneur. Simon Whistler, who'd been an integral part of my initial Multi-Author Facebook Event, just so happened to have a hand in my next big idea as well.

When I complained for what was likely the 15th time about my freelance gig barely paying the bills, he had a revelation that would shape every moment between the meeting and the present day. Simon asked me if there was any way I could adapt my freelancing so that it was for authors instead of low-paying publications. My eyes grew wide as my brain processed the possibilities. Within a week, I had a sales page up for my new business: Best Page Forward. I set a low, low price for writing book descriptions for other authors and I prepared to tell my podcast audience about it.

I never could've expected what happened next.

Opening the Floodgates

Despite the fact that our podcast wasn't even in the top three of our market, the announcement of my new service was absolutely incredible. Within a few weeks, I had over 100 orders for book descriptions. My inbox was completely full of PayPal notifications. Before I knew it, my short-term financial woes were a thing of the past and I had podcast interview requests from the top two shows in the industry. It turned out, the skills I'd picked up from the thousands of articles I'd written in the last half-decade made me perfectly suited for the book description biz. Fellow authors loved my work so much that several of them booked over 20 descriptions each. The next two months pushed me past my limits, but they proved that there was a need for my skills in the marketplace. Had I failed to hone my abilities with new and increasingly difficult gigs the previous few years, I never would've been able to demonstrate the expertise that made my business a hit.

After raising my prices twice, my business settled into a reasonable workload, but I knew that it could only go so far as a one-man army. I brought in some help for the first drafts, but I felt like I had an opportunity here to teach my skills. If I could do it in such a way that would bring me more passive income, so much the better. I just wasn't sure of the best way to pull that off.

It was time for me to hit the books.

Getting Trendy

As my business grew by leaps and bounds, there was another trend in my market exploding before my eyes: online courses. Two of my author idols, Nick Stephenson and Mark Dawson, had just launched very successful courses into a market of learning-hungry authors. Both of them were students of the expensive Create Awesome Online Courses training program, a course I'd bought with two friends a few months earlier. I'd already invested the money, but I had yet to put in the time and the work.

With my interviews coming up on The Creative Penn and The Self Publishing Podcast, I knew that I had an opportunity to tap into a wider audience of authors than ever before. Despite having to write dozens of descriptions a week and handle the other aspects of my business, I knew that getting into the course material was an absolute necessity to take advantage of my impending exposure. I made it a priority to go through every module with a fine-toothed comb. I bugged Nick and Mark to make sure I didn't make any mistakes along the way. I set a deadline to record the course, and pushed myself to the point of exhaustion (and laryngitis) to get it all on video.

It was rough. And expensive. And I made plenty of mistakes along the way.

But when the first two-dozen students opened their wallets to take my training program, I knew that all my effort had been worth it.

Over the course of the next year, I brought in over 200 students to Selling for Authors and wrote over 400 book descriptions. I didn't quite reach the heights of my idols, but I earned enough to take a European vacation with my wife and to go drinking with Nick and Mark on the streets of London. I earned enough to start securing a future for my wife and me. I earned enough for us to add to our family, and I can't wait for our first daughter and a variety of new challenges later in 2016.

The True Gifts

My biggest success was the result of putting all my previous lessons together. When things were going well, I didn't rest on my laurels, I took action to keep the good times rolling. I learned all I could about my next set of endeavors and put in the time, money, and effort to make them come to life. I talked myself hoarse and practically pulled my hair out from dealing with the difficulty, but I refused to drop the ball this time.

There are many challenges yet to come for me as an entrepreneur, but now I have a formula to improve my chances of success in anything I do.

1. Learn as much as I can
2. Invest my time, money, and energy
3. Keep it up when times are easy OR tough
4. Challenge myself to grow
5. Look to the success of others to push me to the next level

I think anybody who follows this formula in one way or another is bound to find success. It's never about the tricks or the tactics alone. You need to learn. You need to take action. You need to push yourself.

If you do this even 70% of the time, then before long, you'll have your own success story to tell.

Now go out there and do the work!

Christopher Westra

Christopher Westra is the author of I Create Reality, which is about how to Manifest Your Desires using Holographic Creation. He has also authored 11 other books and now has 8 apps for iPad and iPhone.

He lives in Pleasant Grove, Utah. He and his wife Kim have 9 children. Christopher loves to run up mountains for fun. He has over 170 websites. Two of the most popular are LightisReal.com and GreatMindPowerBooks.com

From Working in a Prison to Being Financially Free

It's been 12 years since starting my own business, and this is my story of financial freedom. 12 books, 175 websites, and 8 apps later, it definitely wasn't easy. But I would do it again!

I've always been interested in how the mind works. My Mom and I used to read psychology and self-improvement books even back when I was a teenager. My high school wrestling coach had us read "Psycho-Cybernetics" in order for us to learn the art of mental rehearsal. Psycho Cybernetics was probably the first book that had a great impact on me, and I internalized the lessons deeply into my mind and body.

Not only did I use the mental rehearsal skills for wrestling, but also for running, test taking, dating, interviewing, college life, and much more. I realized there was something very powerful going on as I imagined scenarios in great detail and with emotion.

In college at BYU, I eventually changed my major to psychology as I simply enjoyed studying about the mind. In particular I studied how we learn new things, and also about conditioning and programming that can prevent new learning. To this day, I love puzzles and mind teasers that work because of how we are conditioned. I believe these puzzles can help us to get beyond our programming and use our mind in a more powerful, conscious way.

Another book came to me in college that amazed me and altered my perspective about the world. This book was "Time and Free Will", by Henri Bergson. It's not an easy read. He won the Nobel

Prize for Literature in 1927. He was one of the most influential philosophers of his day, and was a very public figure where he lived (in France). His lectures drew huge crowds.

The main idea of the book is that there is no "Time" as we think of it. If there were time (as commonly thought of, modeled after space, like points on a line), then we would not have free will at all. Our human behavior would be deterministic. Free will would be an illusion. Many people actually believe that this is the case.

Bergson encourages you to live freely, with authenticity, and says this can only be done when you let go of the idea of linear time. This book later became the inspiration for my own book on <u>Living in Holographic Time (icreatereality.com/time.html)</u>.

Ever since I was a boy I wanted to have my own business one day. After I graduated from BYU in Psychology, I got married and wrote my first book. It was actually a book on medicinal plants, and how to find and gather them from the wild. I wrote this before the advent of the Internet. Believe me, the Internet makes writing books so much easier! For my book on medicinal plants, I actually had to do research the old fashioned way, in the library.

The book really didn't go anywhere, though I did submit it to publishers. I worked in counseling jobs at a hospital, and later at a prison, for many years, playing with ideas and dabbling here and there in writing. I have always read widely, and continued to do so.

Then in January 2004 I read a couple other books that changed my life in a huge way.

The first was "The Holographic Universe", by Michael Talbot. The subtitle is "The Revolutionary Theory of Reality" and it really is quite revolutionary. This book is an easy read, so get it on Amazon and learn from it. For me, the explanation of the holographic universe let me know that my detailed mental "rehearsals" (my imagined scenarios), were actually real. They were blueprint holograms made of incipient matter.

This is why my imagined scenarios tended to become "clothed" with physical reality and play themselves out on a physical level. In my mind, I combined many of the ideas from Psycho Cybernetics with ideas from The Holographic Universe. This combination developed into my own book about manifesting with "Holographic Creation" (icreatereality.com). This book basically wrote itself and was downloaded to me over the course of 48 hours.

I wish all of my books and products and creations would come like that! This book has been my bestseller and the hub of my business. But I must go back and tell you about the fourth book that impacted my life in a great way, and led to the development of my business.

The next book that changed my life was "The Science of Getting Rich", by Wallace Wattles. I was working in a prison at the time, but within a year and a few months I had my own home-based business! I remember the shivers running up my spine as my vision of the future enlarged and changed. What was possible for me literally changed as a result of reading this book, and I've recommended it to tens of thousands of people since that time.

I read that book in January of 2004 and by March of 2005 I had matched my income at the prison and left the prison. I used to tell people that I had a 20-year sentence, but that I got out in 7 years due to good behavior. That was meant as a joke of course, but there was some truth in it.

Every inmate had a cell with a window, yet my office didn't even have a window. The inmates got to go exercise in the yard, while I just worked. I wanted more freedom in my life...!

In January 2004 when I read The Science of Getting Rich, I was ready for change, and ready to make changes in myself. Shortly after reading the book, I had an epiphany of sorts, while lying down in the bathtub. I knew that my life was going to change in major ways. I KNEW I would be creating my own business and leaving the prison very soon.

It was an amazing experience.

The Science of Getting Rich is a very easy read also. I've since built a couple websites giving away the book and the audio. You can get the free audiobook of The Science of Getting Rich right here: freescienceofgettingrichaudio.com.

The next book that I wrote was a book about Raw and Living Foods. It was over 200 pages and I sent it off to publishers. A few publishers were interested but wanted certain parts changed or added. The experience was just way too slow for me.

Then I met a lady who did some online marketing, advertising things with something called "Google Ads". She asked me if I had ever thought about publishing my book as an ebook and marketing it myself online. I had to ask what an ebook was, but soon I learned and had my own website set up promoting my book. I did use those Google Ads, which were amazingly successful at that time.

I could get "clicks" for about five cents each, from people looking up raw foods or related words. So for five dollars I could send 100 people to my sales page. At least one person would buy my book, out of that 100 (on average), so I traded $5 for about $20 profit. I realized that it was just a matter of numbers of interested people that could create financial freedom for me.

So I worked on those numbers!

I quickly wrote my next book (I Create Reality – How to Manifest Your Desires with Holographic Creation - icreatereality.com), and it was even more successful. But I learned that it's not really the number of books that made for sales. It's the traffic that makes the difference. So I also studied Google's Ad system and got really good at keywords and writing ads.

At one time, I maxed out Google's system with the number of relevant keywords that sparked my ads. I think the number was 60,000. This was Google, yet it was still too many for them to track and process. For years I spent an average of $100 a day ($3000 a month) on Google Ads, yet it was well worth it.

I really enjoyed having an automated system. Someone could see my ad in the middle of the night, purchase my book, get the download, and read it, all without my doing anything.

I took my wife to Hawaii for eight days, and during that time I didn't touch a computer or do any work. Yet during those eight days I made $2362 in profit from royalties! That was really fun. I did hire someone to handle any customer service needs.

When you have a digital product, the whole world is your market, and there are a lot of people in the world.

I was grateful for the royalties for another reason also. Starting in 2006 I started to become ill. I went to doctor after doctor, spending thousands on tests and doctor's fees. We looked into sleep apnea, rheumatoid arthritis, multiple sclerosis, Chron's disease, fibromyalgia, irritable bowel syndrome, chronic fatigue, Lyme Disease, and many more.

Every day I was in pain - in my joints and in my intestines. My fatigue was so bad that I had to take four naps during each day just to get through. Many nights when I went to bed, I hoped I would die in the night. In 2008 it started to affect my brain, bringing with it depression and brain fog. I became quite emaciated – I'm 5' 9" and I got down to 123 pounds.

During this time there is NO WAY I could have held a full time job. Yet the royalties from my books continued to come in and keep us going.

I still, as of 2016, haven't found out what I "have". I just focus on being the healthiest I can be, and numerous therapies help me to function daily. I can get quite a bit done in between my rest times, and I've even learned to work lying on the floor, with a phone, iPad, and even a computer propped up on a chair.

One of my favorite life quotes came from The Science of Getting Rich. It's Wallace Wattles' mantra of "Increased Life for all". In fact, the official name of my business is Increased Life. I do believe in Increased Life for All, and one of my personal goals is to affect one billion people in a positive way. I'd say I'm up around ten million so far with all my apps, books, websites, freebies, newsletters, and Kiva loans.

I made the mistake for many years of not learning SEO (Search Engine Optimization) in order to benefit from organic rankings of my sites on Google and other search engines. The reason I kind of ignored it is that I was doing so well with PPC (Pay Per Click) marketing, which costs money but is somewhat quick and easy.

One thing I did well was develop a subscriber list very early on in my business. Even now, my "list" is one of my most powerful assets, and I treat it with care. You could take all my own personal products away and I would still make money from marketing to my subscribers. But if you took away my subscribers, I would make very little from my products. Traffic is what is important.

Sometimes people would ask me what I did for a living and I'd do my best to explain about Internet marketing and ebooks. Often they would ask, "So you can make enough money selling ebooks?" I would reply, "You can make enough money selling pencils for a penny each, if you sell enough of them."

I was amazed at how stable some of my earnings were, as a ratio of how many people I reached. If 1000 people searched the Internet about "Potty Training" and 15 bought my book, then if another 1000 people reached my site, about 15 more would buy. So marketing was a lot about reaching more people.

This became more difficult about 2009 when Google started to raise their prices for their ads. I was priced right out of that advertising medium. So I really had to expand my business into SEO and also into networking with lots of other authors and marketers to do cross promotions.

I used to get all the traffic I wanted at five cents per click, but that didn't last. My subscriber list grew at about 1000 people per month for the first few years of my business, and that was really nice! I was up to 36,000 fairly easily.

Then I've spent the next seven years getting my subscriber list up to about 72,000, with a lot more creativity and work. Sometimes you don't know what changes in the world or the market will affect your business. Keep tabs on what you can, so you can see changes coming and make them into opportunities for your business (and your personal life).

As I networked with other authors and creators around the world, we learned from each other. I have friends in Malaysia, Singapore, Costa Rica, New Zealand, Australia, and the Isle of Man who are receiving royalties from their virtual creations. It's fun to learn about different cultures from people who actually live there. I go days in a row without leaving my property, but I don't feel confined or limited at all. My life is very rich and I can influence people all across the world through the connecting magic of the Internet.

I've also had the opportunity of "training" several boys to work in my business over the years. They have come with different abilities and talents – some had computer skills to start with, and others didn't. Three have been my sons. They help me by handling whatever they can to free up my time for the things that only I can do.

I'm looking to train a new "assistant" now, as the helper I've had for the last four years is leaving to go on a mission. At first I had to teach him every little thing. Now I can tell him which websites to make mobile friendly and he can work for hours without asking me a question. In addition to teaching these boys about how to build a website and use Word and Excel, I try my best to teach them hard work, commitment, perseverance, creativity, problem solving, goal orientation, vocabulary, and much more.

If they simply keep coming, by the time they leave for College they've learned habits and skills and confidence that can help them be successful for life.

Over the years I've thought about creating and marketing a physical product, but I keep coming back to the digital products. There are just so many advantages. Virtual (downloadable) products don't take any money to ship, and they also have no tax (in most countries). People use their own resources (computer space) to download the product. You can sell the same product an unlimited number of times, so the business can scale quickly.

It's not for everyone. I'm grateful for the people who create and build all the physical items we use in the world. But for me it's been a huge blessing to be able to increase life for others through my digital products.

Even after I've sold a book 10,000 times, I still OWN the book. It's still mine. In this way, it's similar to older times when only the royalty earned royalties. That is why they are called royalties, after all.

I remember reading the book Pride and Prejudice, and also seeing the movie. Jane Austen's novels are filled with people who don't have to work for a living. Why don't they work?

The "upper class" in England, France and other countries owned all the land, and received a continuous passive income from the "rent" of the tenants.

Because the people who received these ongoing payments were the Princes, Dukes, and Earls, the payments came to be called "Royalties".

The royalty knew how to "rent" their property yet still retain ownership!

I came to realize that "interest" is a form of royalty also. You are letting other people use your money (rent it for a time), yet you still own it. So I'm quite fascinated by royalties and developed one product called Royalties University (royaltiesuniversity.com) to teach people about it.

The online business has become competitive. There are many products out there and you have to provide value and differentiate your product from others.

In the last year I've started developing apps for iPhone and iPad, and that has been very fulfilling. It's a fun way to reach more people, and it has great potential. So far, my app income does not match the amount of time I spend on it, but I still have the rest of my business to tide me over while I build it up. You can check out all my apps here: icreatelove.com/apps.

There are a tremendous variety of ways to succeed in the Internet World. I know some people who have one product and spend nearly all their time doing joint ventures and working with affiliates. Others, like me, have dozens or hundreds of websites and many products. I prefer to be continually creating, and spending my entire time marketing one product would not be fulfilling to me.

Some marketers are protective of their subscriber list and rarely promote other people's products. And others are more like me and visualize their subscriber list like a big pool with continual inflow and outflow. I may mail to my list more than some, but the vast majority of my promotions are for free content. It's my intention to enrich everyone's life, even those who never buy anything from me. When someone unsubscribes from my list, I don't mind at all.

Keep it fun and center your business around your interests and expertise and how you can help others to live a better life.

Another reason I so enjoy online marketing is that you can truly start on the proverbial "shoestring". At the very beginning of my business, when I was still working at the prison, and with a young family, I could only afford to use $20 from each paycheck on my business. How I treasured that $20 and carefully decided what I needed to invest it in!

There are even more tools available now, than when I got started. Most of the tools are free.

Then later I came into some very successful years. I remember paying down my regular mortgage amount and then adding hundreds more to pay it down quicker, just because I could. It was fun to go on family vacations to Disneyland and Yellowstone, and not be concerned about money.

I still have some health struggles that limit my productive time, and this has taken some toll on my income. I made more in 2008 than I did in 2015. There are always ups and downs along the way.

One of the final thoughts I'd like to finish with is that "Incremental Actions Bring Monumental Results". That's a Christopher Westra original. Each step in itself is quite small. I literally keep track of each task I do every day, on a color-coded chart. This last year I passed 100,000 tasks since January 2004. This keeps me on track doing the productive items (with the color-coding).

My task list also helps me when I'm feeling rotten or I'm having a bad day, or I've experienced a setback. I can do 30 to 35 tasks – no matter what, and I choose those tasks that move me consistently, even if slowly, toward my major goals. When a project or goal seems too big for me to handle, I divide it into smaller tasks. I realize that when I'm feeling blocked, it's usually because I haven't divided the project into small enough action steps.

Keep up those Incremental Actions. Let no day go by without taking some concrete steps toward your dreams.

Christopher Westra

P.S. You can get loads of Free Classic Manifesting Books right here (at GreatMindPowerBooks.com), and you can also get free beautiful Light Cards and Articles at LightisReal.com.

Dragos Roua

Dragos is a serial online entrepreneur, author, blogger, ultrarunner, tanguero, father and risk taker. He thinks happiness is a process, not a goal. He wrote and self-published 9 books so far, but he thinks you will greatly enjoy this one: <u>Being A Digital Nomad</u> (beingadigitalnomad.com).

3 Different Kinds of Freedom

Freedom. The final frontier.

You know what follows from now on: a long list of catchy phrases narrated in low voice, with the sole purpose to create a context for you to be transported into another world, possibly on another planet, from another galaxy. In a universe where everything is different, and, probably, much more likely to fulfill you fantasies.

Alas, it's not going to be that way. We're not going into another galaxy. We're not going to fantasize about anything in this chapter. We're going to be so realistic, that it may get boring at times. Yet, the outcome of the stories that I'm going to tell is nothing short of Sci-Fi.

There are many types of freedom. As many as feelings of being trapped, I would dare say. No such feeling is identical with another, even in the same person. You may feel trapped because of financial shortage, because of you can't speak freely or because you can't buy whatever you want, whenever you want.

What follows is my story of finding (and enjoying) 3 types of freedom: freedom from an oppressive political regime (communism, that is), freedom from a limited work environment (creating my own company, that is) and freedom to chose the lifestyle that I want (becoming, and still being, at the time of writing this chapter, a digital nomad).

Fast Rewind 27 Years Ago

It's the fall of 1989 and I'm in my hometown, Ramnicu-Valcea, a small city in the center of Romania, near the Carpathian Mountains. At that time I was just admitted to the Faculty of Letters from the University of Bucharest, after a difficult exam (we were 6 people fighting for a place). I was the first on the list, out of more than 400 trying. And I was enjoying that breakthrough big time, because I knew that in 2-3 months I had to serve as soldier. At that time, military service was compulsory.

At that time, also, I lived under a totalitarian, communist regime, led by a dictator called Ceausescu. The food was scarce, the political police, Securitate, was stronger than ever, you couldn't travel outside of the country and cars were permitted on roads every other weekend. Gas, when available, was very expensive. And not everybody could afford a car. It was a sinister way of life, but, since I didn't experience anything else, I could only imagine what it would be to live in a different country.

Every once in a while I was hearing rumors about people fleeing the regime. Some of them (apparently many of them) were caught and had to spend a lot of time in prison, or forced to work at the hideous communism monuments, like Ceausescu's House of People (second biggest building in the world, after Pentagon).

In October 1989 I took a train to Timisoara, the city where I was sent to serve as a soldier. I had 9 months ahead of me, that was the extent of the service for those who were admitted to a college, like me. The rest of us had to serve one year and nine months.

I considered myself lucky. 9 months. It's just 9 months and it will soon be over. I can cope with 9 months.

But in just 2 months something completely unexpected exploded and irreversibly transformed my life and the life of other 20 millions of Romanians.

The events are known now as the Romanian Revolution. It was also the first televised revolution ever. People were out on the streets, asking Ceausescu to leave. It was unheard of, it was unbelievable. Soldiers like us were sent on the streets, in an attempt to suppress the revolution.

We didn't have any information about what's actually going on. Because, for a significant amount of time, the army was sill loyal to Ceausescu, all the information that was reaching us was carefully censored. When the first fight alarm was triggered, we thought we were going to the Hungarian border, because "there was an invasion".

I was in the army for only two months. Only one shooting exercise. I knew my weapon very well and I did well in that shooting exercise, but many of my colleagues didn't. We weren't prepared to be soldiers. We were just kids waiting for those 9 months to pass, waiting to get back to our lives as students.

Since the first alarm until the Ceausescu escape from the roof of the Central Committee building, exactly 6 days and 5 nights passed.

I didn't sleep for a second, during those days and nights. Not even one second.

But those nights shaped my life in such a profound way that even now, after 27 years, I still enjoy the benefits.

Yes, there are benefits in being exposed to tough stuff. Because you get tougher. It's not pleasant to go through tough stuff. It's not sane, you get hurt and you remain with scars at many levels.

But you learn a lot about what you can and what you cannot control in your life.

During those nights, I had only one thought: "I will make it through this. I will get out of this alive. I don't know what it is, I don't know why is this happening to me, but I'll make it. I'll stay alive."

Now let me zoom in a little more, to give you a little bit of context.

The 5 Nights of the Most Beneficial Nightmare of My Life

On December 16th 1989, a military exercise known as "guard" was scheduled for my platoon. "Guard" was the only war mission during peace: we had to guard the perimeter of the base, on certain key points: the fuel depot, the ammunition depot and so on.

The total duration of the mission was 3 days (because we were basically students, we weren't allowed to do more than 3 days of guard per month, the other soldiers were doing much more, sometimes a few months in a row).

We were training for this mission for about a month, with reconnaissance missions, one shooting exercise and a lot of psychological work. The guard meant that we were on duty for 3 hours, then we had to stay awake for another 3, then go to sleep for 3 hours. Rinse and repeat.

It was only 3 days, but it was tough.

On December 15th, a day before the start of the mission, we were allowed to go out in the city, to "relax". Of course we got drunk (that was pretty much everything you could do "out in the city" those days). We got back at the base very late and we got, of course, punished. We were given two options: fuel depot or ammunition depot. Those were the most difficult and risky posts in the entire base. I chose the ammunition depot. I was assigned to the 13th post. Lucky one, I'd say.

We went to sleep and then the next day, at 3PM, the mission started. I was escorted to my post, which was one of the 4 corners of a rectangle containing the ammunition depot. I was seeing the road to the base and a part of the city (we were like 4-5 km away, but we could still see the outskirts of Timisoara).

And so it began. Nothing special happened during my first shift. I got back after three hours, stayed awake another three but couldn't go to sleep the next 3, so I remained awake.

My next shift started exactly at midnight.

And that's precisely when the Romanian Revolution started as well. I heard rumors of soldiers going out (that was not planned, so what the fuck is going on?). Then the shift was doubled, meaning I had to stay in my post until 6AM, not until 3 AM. I was getting sleepy, but at the same time I was quite pumped, because I didn't know what was happening.

As I got back to the base in the morning, I saw a completely changed base. The real fight alarm was triggered (not the exercise alarm) and so there were soldiers everywhere and it was chaos.

Some were saying we're going to the Hungarian border, some were saying there were riots in the city. I didn't have the concept of "riot". People didn't use to get on the streets those times because the punishment was basically instant.

Yet, there were people on the streets.

That night was replicated 4 more times, with an increased intensity. There were a few additions, like more soldiers in the perimeter, or a dog giving birth to puppies, or a gypsy passing by with a chariot, or somebody breaching the perimeter without knowing it, triggering somebody to shoot and so on.

I won't give you all the details, because it will make an entire novel. I just wanted to give a bit more context.

As I was walking along the sides of that rectangle, in the dark that was torn apart every once in a while by a bullet or by a TAB cannon, all I could think was: "I am getting out alive from this".

The first thing that I tried to understand was the extent of the problem. With all the information that I had, I thought we are going into a civil war. And a civil war could last, in my opinion, at least 6 months. So I mentally put myself in the position of having to stay in that perimeter for 6 months.

"If that's what is going to take, then I'd better prepare for it. 6 months. 6 months is not that long. I can do 6 months."

That was probably the first main encounter between yours truly and the sheer truth that we can't control anything but our own reaction to events. It was a brutal encounter, but one that proved beneficial many times in my life.

We live with the wrong assumption that we can directly control our environment. We can't. It's an illusion. There are forces at work much bigger than we can understand.

What we can control, however, it's our reaction to the environment. That thing, we have full control over it. And, if you come to terms with it, you soon realize it's a very powerful thing.

During those nights in Timisoara I learned the first powerful lesson of my life: you can't control what's happening to you, but you can control your reaction to it.

In just a few days, Ceausescu was caught and executed. In two weeks, everything was back to normal. No civil war, no nothing. And just 6 months after I started the compulsory military service, I could go back home, my service was shortened.

The only thing that was changed was that, now, we were free. Like really free. We could travel, we could talk we could start our own businesses.

There were soon other challenges to be fought, like finding a job and making enough money to get by, but that's the topic of the next two parts.

From "Waiting for My Wage" To "I'll Pay Your Wages, Guys"

A few things happened during the next 10 years: I graduated from the Faculty of Letters of the University of Bucharest, I read a few books, drank a few import beers, made a few bucks and, the most important of all, I started a job as a radio anchor.

It was the era of FM radio.

One day, as a student of the Faculty of Journalism (yeah, I did 2 years there as well, just because it was possible) I went to see an FM radio studio. It was just near the faculty building and I heard they were looking for people.

The visit was very exciting, people running the radio were actually our age and they told me to try putting together a few news on paper and come in the afternoon, for the news bulletin. I went to the library, read that day's papers, created a news bulletin not bigger than 4 news and got back at 5:55 PM. The news were scheduled at 6PM.

They asked me: "Would you mind reading the news?" "Like live?" I answered. "Yeah, live."

"Ok, I said".

And that's how I became a radio anchor.

It turned out that my voice was good for that. Never knew it, never even tried to imagine that, but when they first heard me, those guys said it was obvious.

I started a 7 years long career in the mainstream "spoken" media. I had quite a few breakthroughs. For a while I was even in a managing position, hiring people, putting together radio segments and so on.

But something was wrong. It was clear that there was a big gap between reality and media even from the first days, but for a few years, I didn't mind that gap. I was doing my job and, when I wasn't, I was numbing myself with consistent quantities of alcohol.

The salary was way above the average, but so was my lifestyle.

And it wasn't until I reached my 29th year of life that the obvious gap between what I wanted to do and what I was doing had to be confronted.

At that time the salary started to pour in slower and slower. The company I was working for had troubles and money were scarce. I remember there were queues of dozens of people waiting for hours to pick up their wage. It didn't smell good.

So, after around one year of struggling with low payments, internal conflict and a lot of confusion about my life, I realized I don't want to do that.

From the moment of realization until the moment of clearly defining what it was missing I think there were quite a few months.

I mention this (and I insist upon this) in order to support those of you who are struggling right now.

It's ok to be confused. It's normal. Once you are so habituated with a certain lifestyle, even the definition of a new one is challenging, let aside the actual steps to change something. So, don't rush. Stay in that awareness, be there, observe, take into account, journal, define, scratch, start over and define again.

There's a certain inertia plaguing our lives and we must learn to accept it.

Thing is I realized, after this long and tiring process, that, once again, I was not free.

My prison was now the fact that I was selling my time for something I didn't believe in. And for much less money that I thought I was worth of.

Escaping that prison proved to be a much longer task than the Romanian Revolution. It didn't happen in a week. It took me almost two years to go from being an employee to have my own company.

The Overlapping Process

If I would have to define now the process, I would call it "the overlapping process". It's a term borrowed from Sean Wes (a nice guy teaching about entrepreneurship these days).

In short, going from being an employee to being an entrepreneur, consists in creating enough of a "cushioning" to support you during the first bumpy years. I didn't use the exact terms at that time, all I knew was that I have to find way to support myself.

So, I quit my radio anchor job and worked for a small software company that was looking for a quality assurance engineer. I wasn't an engineer, but the company didn't exactly needed one, but a person who was tech savvy and able to speak and write French (all of their clients were French). I graduated from the Faculty of Letters with a degree in French literature, mind you.

My task was to test apps and to write test reports.

I was soon to find out that the quality assurance is not the most popular guy in the room. Programmers kinda feared me, because I was the guy hunting for bugs. But that subtle isolation was very good.

I had my own small office, in which I was testing for a few good hours the software and then I was free to read about what I was interested in.

And so I started to learn programming. From the first salary I bought a big book about Borland C++ and I was reading it during the 30 minutes commute from my studio in the outskirts of Bucharest to the headquarters of the software company.

I also read during breaks. Or home, at nights. In a few months, I knew Borland C++.

I never used Borland C++. But the fact that I became savvy at the whole tech thing was hugely beneficial.

I also bought a computer. It was a Pentium at 90Mhz, with a 5Gb hard-disk. I don't remember very clear, but I know I overclocked it for 133Mhz and I thought this was a big deal.

Having a computer allowed me to test, to learn, to improve.

The "overlapping" technique means supporting yourself for long enough until you are able to jump in the pool. And that's exactly what I did during that year.

After I learned enough and after I built enough confidence, I decided to start a company. I decided to jump into the pool.

My first company was created with two partners. We found out really soon that we were not very compatible and we were able to part ways in a peaceful way. There were some fights but mainly because of the stress, not because of the persons.

To make a long story short, when I was 29, I created my first company. It was focused on building websites (it was 1999 and the web was starting to become a big thing). After two years of building websites for clients I decided to start creating some websites for us. We picked a few niches (cars, food and few others) and started to slowly build vertical portals.

The money from building websites were enough to support to building process and, 4 years after founding the company, I was able to cut the client work and focus only on the products we built ourselves.

Again, I share all these numbers in order to give you some comparable figures. It may or it may not take that long to you. You may be better prepared than me, or you may be in a better position, financially speaking, but bottom line is, all good things take time.

The Second Prison

7 years after I started the company I had another breakthrough. Although I was skilled in the processes, although I was pretty good at what I was doing, I discovered a different type of prison.

I was tied up to my own creation.

I was so involved in the business that I couldn't find time for myself. My personal life was a mess (I had already one divorce and two kids with whom I was barely spending any time, and the second divorce was starting to look quite possible). I was having frequent depression episodes and gaining a lot of weight. I was burned out.

At that time I started to be interested - as a necessary countermeasure to my own personal mess - in personal development. I started to read a lot on the topics and spend a lot of time on watching movies or starting experiments in that area, sometimes at the expense of my business managing tasks.

The size of the business I created, or, to be more specific, the compound size of the tasks I was taking upon me was way bigger than I was willing to admit. From the outside, I was looking like a successful entrepreneur and, from any angle, my company was very successful. But the price I was paying was too big for me.

I needed a way to scale down.

As I got more and more immersed in the world of self-improvement, I started to understand more about myself and about what I was doing. I realized that continuing on that path, of scaling up the business, while finding a way to scale down my involvement, was an impossible task.

So, after another tormenting year, I finally decided I want to sell. The numbers were good, the products competitive and we had two market leaders (our cars and food portals were basically leading the way at that time).

After I took the decision, things unfolded much easier. In about 9 months I found not one, but two buyers. During the due diligence process one of them dropped out, but the other went through and, 9 years after starting my first company, I did my first successful exit.

So, my second prison was made up by myself. Carefully, day by day, task by task, I created such an oppressive work environment for myself, by loading into my system enormous amounts of work, that, at some point, I had to stop.

I know that many of you are very eager to start their own business, in order to "escape the 9 to 5 prison". I think this is legit.

But be very, very careful not to overdo this. Be very careful not to end up with another prison, much more elusive (because it is closely tied up with feelings of joy and satisfaction, probably with self respect) and much more difficult to escape from.

To make (another) long story short, after I became my own boss, I realized I need to do more. More? What more?

The Third Prison

In 2008, the real estate bubble was at its peak in Romania. House prices were sky-rocketing and I was caught in the process. We already bought a house in the newly enriched outskirts of Bucharest and I thought the bubble is still going up. I didn't even think it was a bubble.

After I sold my company, I was floating around. There were money in the bank and I thought I was invincible. I continued to put money in real estate and started a self-improvement blog, as a way to keep myself busy. To test the waters and, who knows, maybe to start something new.

After 2008 I had two very well-deserved decompression years. Alas, one thing that started way before 2008, the decay of my second marriage, consumed its end in 2009.

So here I am, a successful entrepreneur, freshly divorced, living in a luxurious house, with two expensive jeeps at the gate.

And once again unhappy.

The third prison is also the subtlest one. It's a prison of a certain lifestyle. And lifestyle is such an elusive concept. It's so hard to grasp it.

That's why, probably, the third prison was the most consuming one. I was way too attached to my image of a successful entrepreneur, to my possessions, to my social status. I identified so much with it (especially after the burn out of running my first business) that parting way with that seemed impossible.

And yet, it had to be done.

Although I was, by any definition, a successful person, I felt like somebody else. I didn't want to get back to the business world, as I knew it. I found it too consuming and too depressing.

I started to focus on the blog and to slowly reach a sustainable audience. The experience I gathered in those 9 years of web development soon became relevant and the blog took off. (Right now, my blog is constantly mentioned in top 100 self-improvement blogs for the last 3 years.)

At the same time, the real estate bubble was exploding. By 2010 it was obvious, once again, that there was a gap between what I thought is the value of the house I was living in (and the associated expenses) and what it really was.

In other words, I lost money. A shitload of money.

Almost all the money I made from the exit.

So, in 2011, I decided to leave. I rented a small apartment in Bucharest and put the house for rent. I still remember the day where I actually left with just a handful of stuff and didn't even look back.

I wasn't leaving behind only an overpriced house, still owned by the bank and devaluated to almost half of what I paid for. I was leaving behind another me.

A "me" way too attached to his personal image, a "me" weighing 20 kilos more than normal, a "me" without anything to offer in a personal relationship. A "me" with whom I didn't want to hang out, to be honest.

In 2011 I started a new escape. This time it was even slower than the second one.

I started to run. I was very bad at it, partly because I was overweight, partly because I was too egotistic to actually look for advice. As a result, the progress was slow and I was injured very often.

I started to work from coffee shops and to provide business coaching. The scaling down, or the "downshifting" of my life was impressive. I went from spending 5-6000 EUR per month, to only 1500-2000. I just realized I didn't need that much.

And that the effort and the cost of maintaining that amount of spending was simply not I wanted. I didn't want that life. And I wasn't that person anymore.

I valued more my freedom, my flexibility, and my time.

I slowly got back to spend time with my kids, as much as I could, although none of them was living with me.

I took tango lessons and I even taught tango for half a year.

At the beginning of October 2012 I ran my first marathon. It was a grueling experience. But one that, in a sense, cured me.

I was slowly building a new identity.

I was now a digital nomad, a person working from place to place, enjoying a healthy lifestyle and balanced relationships.

I continued to run and, soon, I realized I enjoy running distances way longer than the marathon.

I ran my first 100km in 2015 and one month later I finished a 222km long race in Hungary.

Meanwhile, while I was working in coffee shops, I started a networking event, called Open Connect. Since 2012 until today, I kept more than 200 events (which means pretty much every Thursday, except legal holidays). Around the event, a nice, 5000+ people community gathered organically.

And on top of that community, with the help of two angel investors, a coworking hub was created, Connect Hub. That's the business I run for the last two years. Still bumpy, but way better than what I used to do.

I'm in Connect Hub right now, writing these words and two weeks ago I ran a 24 hours race in Timisoara, the city where I escaped my first prison, 27 years ago.

I lost 20 kilos and people who didn't see me in the last 5 years can barely recognize me. I look like in my twenties. And I feel even better than that.

I am free and I feel free. I don't need to prove anything to anyone, I'm not attached to anything (not even to Connect Hub, I'm ready to quit anytime, if something doesn't work anymore) and I enjoy a beautiful relationship for 3 years now.

The pressure of coping with the demands of society in terms of "being successful" can lead you to a dead end. The dead end of standard images of success. The dead end of been wealthy but unhappy. The dead end of identifying yourself with false images at the expense of forgetting who you really are.

This dead end, this third prison, is the most elusive one. It's hard to give up your image of a successful entrepreneur and start working in coffee shops. It's hard to leave behind your half a million EUR lifestyle standard. It's really hard.

But once you gather the strength to get out of the illusion, you will get your real life back.

Instead Of Conclusion

The winding road to freedom is never simple, nor it is straight and easy. Probably because, as you saw, the mere definition of freedom is never simple, straight or easy.

Becoming free is a convoluted process in which, most of the time, you have to give something for something more, you have to trade your current comfort for something that may or may not be fulfilling in the near future.

But is it in this process that all the value is to be found. It's not the milestones you are reaching, although, in hindsight, they will make quite some nice stories for your grand-children (or for people reading collective books, for instance, grin, grin). In the end, the only thing that counts is the actual journey.

Probably you'll understand now what I mean when I say: happiness is a process, not a goal.

Thanks for reading my chapter. If you'd like to learn more from me, please visit my website at www.DragosRoua.com. Thank you.

Henri Junttila

Henri Junttila runs the popular blog, WakeUpCloud.com, and has been helping people find and follow their passion since 2009. He helps people through his articles, videos, books, courses, training, and coaching.

From Passion to Purpose and Building Confidence

Do you wish that you could follow your passion, and do what you love, but you're held back by your fears?

I've been there. In fact, when I started following my passion, I was overwhelmed with doubt, fear, and anxiety.

My journey begins with a wish for doing what I truly love. But I'm held back by thoughts of not being good enough. I wonder if I have what it takes.

As you keep reading, you will discover how I was able to keep moving forward despite the internal oppression I experienced. You will also see how doing what I loved paid off, and how it led to a passionate life.

2006: Failure

My journey begins in 2006. All I had was a notion of wanting to make a living online. I didn't know what I was going to do. I didn't know how. I just knew that it felt exciting.

I didn't know anything about marketing, writing, networking, or even the technology involved. I had built a few websites when I was 14, but that didn't translate well.

At the time, I was a professional poker player, and had been since 2004. My zest for poker was fading. I felt it was time to move on.

I wanted to succeed fast. I was in a hurry. So I paid someone to build a site for me on golf. (I used to play a lot of golf when I was younger). That site never gained momentum, because I didn't know what to do after the site was built. Plus, it wasn't really my passion.

After that, I looked for the next quick fix, which was internet marketing coaching. I thought that I had finally found the answer. They made big promises, and I believed them. After six months, I had spent over $10.000 with no revenue to show for it. I had a website on poker, but the taps weren't turned on, so to speak.

I came away from the experience feeling despondent. I was ready to give up. And I did stop trying for a few months. However, eventually the fire within me returned. I knew this was the path, and I knew there was a way.

Going through all of this planted a seed within me that I needed to take responsibility for my own success, but it wasn't yet time for that seed to bloom.

After spending $10.000 on coaching and website building services, I was looking for more information. I fell for get rich quick programs. I bought courses, books, workshops. Anyone who promised me success, I was in.

I don't regret this first year, because it taught me what didn't work. It was hard to go through, because I had high expectations, but I had to learn the hard way that progress doesn't happen overnight, especially if I have no previous experience.

2007: Rebellion

As 2007 rolled along, I was still trying different tools, methods, and programs. I was trying to get traffic to my poker website. I was attempting to get something going.

I didn't notice it at the time, but my mindset was gradually shifting. I began looking for solutions that required work, instead of falling for get-rich-quick schemes. Once I began studying and emulating what worked, I started seeing the possibility of success.

Nevertheless, I was still uncertain about where I was going. I was afraid, because I didn't feel good enough. Who was I to build a website, and share what I knew, when so many others were better, smarter, and more experienced?

I swung between hope and fear. Luckily I had a few tools that helped me get through these tough times. I had bumped into *The Power of Now* by Eckhart Tolle in 2005 during a trip to Thailand. I was meditating regularly. I also attended a Neuro-Linguistic Programming (NLP) training with Richard Bandler in London.

I was learning more about how the mind works, which is a recurring theme in my life. I was beginning to see how I wasn't experiencing life directly. I was experiencing life through my thoughts. The thoughts I believed gave me a flavor of life.

And daily meditation helped me step back and observe how my mind worked. I was less caught up in my mind. Instead, I was a witness to it. These were still early days, so I was still struggling and suffering, but not as much as I used to.

I was taking in information that helped me. I was doing some of the right things, which alleviated some of the struggle.

This was also the year I met my girlfriend, who today is the mother of my children. Meeting her pulled me away from trying to succeed, which sounds bad, but it turned out to be a good thing.

2008: Ready to Give Up

After two years of trying, I was ready to throw in the towel, and I did just that for most of 2008. I was looking for meaning in other places. I felt empty. I was trying to escape that feeling by looking outside. I thought I wanted to become a doctor, to travel, to do something, anything.

I was looking for something that always existed within me. All my running only kept me stuck, like trying to get out of pit of quicksand.

But this year was a blessing in disguise. Although I was running, I was also taking a break from trying to succeed. I wasn't pushing as much. I made a living playing poker. I spent time with my new girlfriend.

Looking back, this level of detachment was precisely, and paradoxically, what I needed in order to move forward. To my surprise, things started happening on their own.

One day, I looked at the emails from my poker website, and I noticed people wanted to advertise. So I began selling advertising. "I have nothing to lose," I thought.

Throughout 2008, more and more advertising requests dropped in, and I did my best to make deals.

Even though I wasn't seeing the success I thought I should have, I was moving forward. Each step was leading to the next. All I had to do was relax, and trust my excitement.

Later in 2008, my girlfriend and I traveled to Peru to attend an ayahuasca ceremony. We flew to the Amazonian Rainforest, where we spent a week. Now, I don't know if that trip made the difference, or not. But I know that it set me up for what was to become a breakthrough year in 2009.

2009: Breakthrough

The seed that was planted in 2007 was beginning to bloom. I began to feel empowered. I realized that I had to find my own way. I couldn't rely on a system or method. I could learn, but ultimately I had to trust my own inner guidance.

Around February of 2009, I began running into people who were building websites that were making money. What was the secret? They packed their websites full of valuable information. In other words, there was no secret, only hard work.

They looked for the intersection between what they loved and what was profitable. I had experienced digestive issues when I was in my teens. I began building a website on that topic.

The website service I was using was called Site Build It. They provided all the tools I needed to run my website. They also provided a step-by-step guide on what I needed to do to succeed.

Remember, at this time I'd gone through three years of trying and failing. I was sick of looking for shortcuts. I just wanted to work. I'd finally found something where people were succeeding. And I knew that if I worked hard enough, I would see results.

I didn't care how much money I made. I just wanted to make something, anything. Even a few hundred per month would've been a success, because it would prove that I could do this.

Around April of 2009, I quit playing poker cold turkey. I wanted to put all my attention into building my website. I put all my time into my website for three to four months. And I began seeing results. I was suddenly making $500 per month from advertising and recommending products I found helpful.

At this point, I bumped into another way of making money online that played well with my skill-set.

The teacher seemed honest and trustworthy. I contacted a few of the students. They were thriving, so I decided to jump in.

The details of what it was aren't as important, because it doesn't work as well today as it did back in 2009. Suffice it to say, I wrote articles that sent people to a website where I recommended a product I liked. This is called affiliate marketing.

I now put all my focus on making this work. I wrote thousands of articles during the course of a few years. I even hired writers to help me as my income increased.

At the end of 2009, I was making over a thousand dollars per month from my website and affiliate marketing. That may not seem like much, but I lived a simple life. It was enough for me.

And more than that, it showed me that I could make a living following my excitement.

2009 was when I was truly ready to make something happen. I stopped chasing quick fixes, and I stopped scattering my energy. I realized that if I wanted to succeed, I had to focus on one thing at a time, and put in the work.

In order to do that, I needed to find something that resonated with me, something that I loved. And I found that with my first website on stomach health. With affiliate marketing, I focused on health as well. Health has always been a passion of mine. I've always enjoyed writing, so I used that to help me create websites and write articles.

At this point, I was making enough money, so I began looking for more. I was no longer satisfied with just building more websites. I wanted to expand the excitement and fulfillment in my life.

That meant sharing my journey of personal development with others. Blogging had interested me for a long time. I didn't just want to make money. I wanted to contribute, and to share what I had discovered.

But once again, doubts crept up. I didn't believe I was ready. Maybe sharing my story was something I could do when I was making more money. Perhaps then I could have the credibility so people would listen.

Luckily, I came across a coach who told me that I didn't have to make more. I just had to share my story. I didn't have to know everything, or be an expert, to share my tale.

Still, I procrastinated. Doing what I truly loved brought out the monsters within me. Yet I knew that this was what I wanted deep down.

But I kept putting it off until, one night, I had a dream. I remember a voice saying: "Start now."

I woke up startled. I've never experienced anything similar since, but I can still remember that voice. I don't know why, but that dream sparked something within me. I began my next journey.

It was in November of 2009 that I came up with the idea of Wake Up Cloud, my blog. I didn't know how I was going to make money. All I wanted to do was share what I knew.

Meanwhile, in December of 2009, my girlfriend and I decided to travel to Spain. And it's in Spain that 2010 kicks off.

2010: Doing What I Love

We traveled to Fuengirola, which is in southern Spain.

I was still working on my health websites. I even helped my girlfriend build a small income stream. We also built other smaller websites, but they never really gained traction. The excitement wasn't there.

My focus was on Wake Up Cloud. I had joined a course by Chris Garrett called Authority Blogger.

Are you beginning to notice a pattern in my successes? I find someone that resonates with me, I learn from them, and I take massive action in whatever way I can.

In Authority Blogger, I once again had a step-by-step plan laid out. I didn't follow it exactly. I noticed the parts that felt magnetic to me, and I took action.

My confidence was building, because I knew I could make a living. I'd already done it. Now the question was: What was the right path for me to build my blog?

The right path revealed itself by what was magnetic and exciting to me. As I went through the course, I picked out what I could do, and what resonated.

Within a few months, and a lot of work, I had built a blog with over 1.000 subscribers.

At this point I began to notice that I didn't have to be as rigid in following every step of the course I was in. I could experiment, and see what worked for me. And once I found what worked, I doubled down on it, and that amplified the results.

To do this, I had to trust my inner navigational system. I was beginning to notice that life had a flow. There was something within me that I could trust. I didn't have to have it all figured out.

As my readership grew, I began receiving questions from my readers, such as:

"How are you able to make a living and live abroad?"

"How did you overcome your fears?"

"What tools do you use to run your business?"

"How did you find your passion?"

I began answering these questions through my articles. Eventually I realized that it wasn't enough. So I created my first ebook on living a passionate life. I sold it for $9.95. It sold around 50 copies in its first month. Not groundbreaking, but it was a step in the right direction for me.

I gradually realized that maybe my mind didn't know what it was talking about. In other words, I had thoughts about not being good enough, but each time I challenged those thoughts, and I took another step, I realized that I was good enough.

I ran into fear about not being a writer. But I stayed focused on taking one step at a time. With each step, I was seeing through the illusion of my thoughts.

After my book on living a passionate life, I decided to create a product on how I was doing affiliate marketing. I wanted to challenge myself, so I didn't just write an ebook; I recorded videos, conducted interviews, and created other extras to help people succeed.

Once again, I sold about 50 copies during launch, but at a higher price point. I was slowly gaining confidence. I saw that I didn't have to create perfect products. I didn't have to know everything. I just had to solve a problem for people.

During this time, I also experimented with coaching and consulting. I didn't do much of it. But I did enough to dip my toes outside my comfort zone.

2010 was a year of opening up my perspective. We were in Spain, eating good food, making new friends, and learning Spanish. But after almost a year in Spain, I felt it was time to return to Finland.

When I say that I felt like it was time, what I am describing is a shift of energy. It feels like a magnetic pull towards something. It's not the anxious searching of the mind. Instead, it's a gentle nudge from the heart.

2011: Struggling

In 2011, I returned to struggling. The energy for my older websites was waning. I wasn't as interested in them. I wanted to make Wake Up Cloud my main income source.

I was right in where the energy was going, but I was in a hurry. I was trying to push the pace of life, and it led to anxiety and fear. This was a year of transition, and transitioning can be rocky.

I began working with a business coach, and he helped me gain clarity on what I wanted to do, and how to make my vision a reality.

I returned to exploring Neuro-Linguistic Programming (NLP), but from different teachers. I was also deeply drawn into meditation, and being in the present moment. I was diving deep into my inner world, looking at my fears, beliefs, and thoughts. At this point, I had meditated regularly for half a decade, but something drew me deeper.

I then used what I had learned—in NLP and my self-exploration—to coach others. I did some free coaching, just to learn more, and see how I could help.

Then I stumbled onto a writing gig with one of the biggest personal development blogs in the world. It brought in extra income.

In retrospect, this year went fine. It was my trying to force progress that added more anxiety than was needed. If I had relaxed, I would've enjoyed the journey that much more.

And in December of 2011, my first son was born, which was both amazing, and scary. It put pressure on me to bring in income. At the same time, it began opening up something within me. I didn't feel like a father, yet I felt that side of me being pulled out. The birth of my son didn't affect my mindset much. I still followed my excitement and passion.

I worked on upgrading my ebook on passionate living. I updated, added interviews, audios, and workbooks. And I raised the price, because it was now a course, not just a book. I launched the new version in 2012.

I was still unsure about where things were going, but I was taking small steps. I was doing what I could with what I had, and that was enough.

2012: Gaining Momentum

There was no big launch for the new version of passionate living. I did a tele-seminar series. I had never conducted a tele-seminar, so I thought I would try it. If I remember correctly, I sold 20 copies, and then things returned to normal sales-wise.

I enjoyed creating the new version, because when I re-wrote and re-recorded it, I was in a meditative place, so the new version was imbued with that. People enjoyed it. And I enjoyed the experience.

2012 was the year of digital products. During this year, I created 4 courses, and upgraded passionate living.

All of the products sold well. I kept doing what worked. I wrote for other blogs. At the same time, I was trying to learn more about marketing.

Once again, I was pushing a bit too hard. I was looking for better results, and I thought better marketing would do it, but it didn't.

I also tried podcasting in 2012 and 2013. While it was fun, it didn't produce better results than what I was doing, so I eventually gave it up. But what it did help me to do was to become more aware of audio quality.

In 2012, I bumped into an honest marketer, and we formed a sort of 2-person mastermind. We never called it that, but we began exchanging emails, and bouncing ideas off of each other. I never looked for this. Instead, it developed naturally by me having fun, and connecting with people.

At the same time, I watched my son take his first step. He was bringing out the playful side in me. I still didn't identify as being a dad, but I enjoyed my little boy.

I keep repeating myself, but my journey has truly been about taking one step at a time. Whenever I've been afraid or worried, I focus on taking one step at a time. I focus on taking another step, and then seeing what unfolds.

When I do that, the path in front of me opens up. As I take one step, another one emerges.

2013: Problems into Opportunities

In the beginning of 2013, I launched my Academy, which was the natural progression from my digital products in 2012.

With my digital products, I gave my readers an example of what a path could look like to doing what you love.

And with my Academy, I took all those digital products, filled in the gaps, and created the next version. Those who bought my products before got either free access or a heavy discount when they joined the Academy.

Once again, you see my step-by-step progression. It all began with a small ebook in 2010. In 2013, I was creating a comprehensive Academy. I did this by listening to the feedback of my customers. I kept asking: How can I help more?

Once I launched the Academy, the members were asking for a forum, so I created another product which was a members-only forum with some other extra material, such as interviews and mini-courses.

However, people were confused, because there were now two similar products: Academy and a members-only forum. At first, I wasn't sure what to do, but as I let it simmer, I eventually asked myself: What would be best for my students?

The answer was to combine the two, so the Academy absorbed the members-only forum with all the extra content. It felt good to me. My students were happy with the change.

I kept creating new lessons for the Academy on a weekly basis, because I was still excited about it. I had the energy to create, and to help my students.

Then in the middle of 2013, books came back into my life. You see, I had been thinking about self-publishing a book for a few years, but tax laws and other hurdles had kept me away.

Now I bumped into a solution. I discovered that there wasn't a tax problem after all. Something had changed that now allowed me to move forward. Life had brought me the next step, which was to write a book.

My first book, *Find Your Passion: 25 Questions You Must Ask Yourself*, was based on one of my more popular blog posts, and to this day, it's my most popular book.

Once more, I found a course. This time on self-publishing. I followed the steps that were relevant to me, and I wrote my book. I then remembered one of my old poker coaches mentioning that he worked with a wonderful book editor. I got in touch with her, and she helped me edit and finish my book.

I would then go on to write several more books. I kept following what made me come alive, and what inspired me.

To me, this is what it means to live my purpose. I follow what excites, interests, and fascinates me. Life brings me what I need, and I keep putting one foot in front of the other.

In September of 2013, we moved into a new house. We'd been living in a small apartment until then, and we needed space, especially with a growing child among us.

Life and business was flowing smoothly, until I was hit with an existential crisis at the end of 2013.

2014: Re-Invention Through Darkness

In early 2014, I was questioning the foundations of everything. Life felt meaningless, hopeless. I could not find comfort in spirituality, meditation, or anything else.

I was lucky, because I had been meditating regularly since 2005-2006. I was able to witness what was going on without getting too caught up in my thoughts.

Nevertheless, it was a tough experience, but it was also enlightening. I learned a lot from going through that dark time. I came out of it looking at my life anew, because I had gone into the darkest places within myself, and I had survived. I discovered that if I can go through that, I can go through anything.

I gained even more clarity on how our thinking creates our experience. As I came out of my journey into darkness, I began recording more videos and sharing them online.

I also finished another one of my books, *Do What You Love: Essays on Uncovering Your Path in Life*.

I kept writing for my blog, my newsletter, and creating courses in the Academy. I played with my son. I watched him grow, cry, laugh, and have fun. I spent a lot of time at home. This was a year of psychological rest for me. Little did I know that the following year would be similar to this one.

2015: Withdrawing from the World

As 2015 came along, I kept improving the Academy. I created more courses. It was a year of improving what had already been created. I didn't have energy to do much. I wasn't motivated for big changes.

Even at this stage in my business, I still battled worry and fear. But I realized that the future is always uncertain, and my mind wants to know what's coming. I kept following what felt magnetic to me, and life kept working out.

I kept surprising myself, because I was never someone who blindly believed that you can do what you love and life will work out. I always wanted to experiment and discover the truth for myself. So I was discovering that that was indeed the case.

Life brought me opportunities. What inspired me, I looked further into. As I relaxed further, life began going more smoothly, because

I was never experiencing life directly. I experienced life through my thoughts, and I didn't have to believe all my thoughts. If I felt anxious or afraid one day, I didn't feel like I had to fix it. I knew it would pass.

In August of 2015, my second son was born. Watching him enter the world is another experience I will never forget. It reminded me of how I am not as in control of life as I believe. I am a part of life, and a part of nature, and life puts me where I need to be, as long as I'm willing to trust it, and follow my excitement.

Sometime during 2015, I began feeling like I didn't want to share anything. I stopped recording videos. I stopped writing new articles. I still created lessons for the Academy. I revised and updated old articles to keep my newsletter subscribers happy. I had hundreds of articles to choose from, so it wasn't a problem.

I respected this next chapter of my life. I knew that there was a time to work, and a time to rest. It seemed it was time to rest.

I spent the rest of the year consuming courses, books, and watching TV-series and movies. I had fun, while going easy on myself.

2016: Shifting & Changing

In the second half of 2016, my energy began to return. I was interested in making videos again. I wanted to work with people 1-on-1. In other words, I was ready to re-enter the world.

The funny thing is that I suddenly started receiving comments on my videos asking me to come back, to make videos on certain topics. That didn't happen during my year off, or I didn't see them.

This is an example of how life works for me. I notice what life is bringing, and where my energy wants to go.

I have no idea if what I've built so far will hold up, or if it will change completely. I'm okay with that level of uncertainty. As an entrepreneur, I have to be.

I've learned to trust my inner guidance system. I've experimented with it for over a decade. I've seen that it knows the way. And the way I trust it is by noticing what I'm interested in, and excited about.

It's simple, but fears and doubts pop up. I worry about the future, about money, about what's going to happen like everyone else. But I don't prioritize my fears. I prioritize following what makes me come alive.

After a year of not wanting to share, my energy is gradually returning, and I feel more inspired to share. But I can only say that it seems that way, because I cannot predict the future, nor do I try to.

My job is to live my life in the present moment, because that is all I can do. I do that by, you guessed it, following my excitement.

Life will have its ups and downs, but that doesn't inherently mean that I must struggle. How I relate to life will determine how much I enjoy the path in front of me.

And the way I relate to life today is vastly different from Henri in 2006. I trust life more. I trust myself more. I have a deeper insight into how I work, and how life works.

So I follow my excitement moment to moment, as best as I can. I write this because I want to. I'm not trying to get anywhere, or to get exposure. I felt inspired to share this with you, so here I am.

Who knows where it will lead, or what comes next. That is the adventure part of life. There is uncertainty, but that uncertainty is what makes life so interesting. You can view uncertainty as a problem, or as an opportunity.

If there's anything I want to leave you with, it's this: Keep taking one tiny step at a time in the direction that excites you the most, even if it scares you.

As you've read my story, you've seen that I wasn't fearless. I simply challenged my thoughts, and I kept putting one foot in front of the other. I kept doing my best, and here I am.

Thank you for reading.

Luke Jones

Luke Jones is a Personal Trainer, Nutritionist and Online Content Creator at Health Room (www. herohealthroom.com), where he explores and shares ideas in healthy living. His goal is to help as many people as possible unlock their potential and unleash their inner hero.

You can catch up with his latest content (and download your free HERO Toolkit) over at herohealthroom.com

Luke also runs online Nutrition Coaching and Personal Training. If personalized, one-to-one support with your diet and lifestyle is something you're after, get in touch to find out more: luke@herohealthroom.com.

The Foundations of Massive Success

It feels a little strange to be sat here writing about my story, with the goal of inspiring someone out there to take action and get to where they want to be in life.

I tend towards the introverted side of the spectrum, so talking about myself has never been a strong point. But then as I finish off the first round of editing, I realize that I've made plenty of mistakes and toiled with enough first world struggles over the past few years to learn a thing or two about what works and what doesn't, in relation to building a successful business.

Even though I'm not currently at a point where I would declare myself financially free, I do feel as if it's a path that I'm heading towards in some shape or form, which is precisely why I was asked to contribute to this great project. Progress has been made, and if I gaze hard enough, the future looks promising.

So as an average Joe and a relative newcomer to this world of building financial freedom, I guess it figures that other average Joes and newcomers out there could extract some value from my story after all. That makes me feel a bit better, so let's get started.

As a Personal Trainer, Nutritionist, and Online Content Creator in the healthy living space, I suppose it makes sense that my tale begins with movement. Human movement that is. Indeed that's where everyone's story starts – whichever way you look at it. But I mean it in a more ideological sense, as opposed to literal.

Ever since I can remember, the practice of human movement has been a central focus in my life. More specifically, my interest falls on the nuances and complexities behind feats of strength, flexibility, endurance, skill, and all-round human performance.

Although I've lost sight of the significance of staying true to my passion a few times, it's always been patiently sitting there in the background - the keystone, holding everything else together.

It all started in the sleepy town I grew up in, near the valleys of South Wales. Close to the wilderness of the mountains, but not too far from the convenience of the city. I was lucky to be brought up with a loving family and a close-knit group of friends, and movement was one of our core bonding points.

Football was initially the main medium. I loved it, and played as much as I could from the time I could walk, until my late teens. There's something special about battling alongside your closest buddies whilst your family watches in support. Words can't quite do it justice.

Hiking, running and climbing trees in the above-mentioned mountains were other big outlets for moving. I dabbled in athletics too, mainly focusing on jumping over poles, sandpits and hurdles.

As I transitioned through my teen years, the movement theme followed me. I became hooked on martial arts, which at the time it seemed like a strange transition to make, but it makes sense now that I look back at it. As a young child, my idols were the Power Rangers and Spiderman – this was just my way of becoming more like them.

It started with Tang Soo Do, and soon evolved to Brazilian Jiu Jitsu, Thai Boxing and Mixed Martial Arts. I trained and competed whenever I could, picking up more than a few injuries on the way.

Lifting weights and performing bodyweight exercises were the next natural progression. They came hand in hand with the martial arts and the goal of becoming the most well rounded athlete that I could be. I strived for general athleticism – being equally comfortable lifting a heavy weight as embarking on a long hike. Striking a balance between all the components of fitness, and being useful in an emergency.

This desire to be a good athlete soon evolved to the goal of becoming the best version of myself. With that I dived down the deep rabbit hole of self-improvement. I devoured everything I could. From strength and conditioning and healthy eating, to mindfulness and recovery techniques, and everything else in between.

It was almost an obsession. I read countless books and article, watched videos and listened to podcasts, acquiring as much knowledge and as many different viewpoints as I could.

By my late teens I knew deep down that this was all I wanted to do with the rest of my life – to learn and practice movement and self-improvement, and share my ideas and findings with others. But I just couldn't figure out *how* to do it. That was the big sticking point.

Anything that did come to mind, I quickly dismissed as being unrealistic, or too risky. It's a bold reflection of the world we live in. Security is the name of the game, and there was no security in a half formed vision. So, like many childhood dreams around the world, the idea was placed on the backburner.

In the meantime, I was working hard at school. As I mentioned above, being a naturally introverted, anxious young lad has its disadvantages. For one, I couldn't talk to anyone other than those closest to me without going a bright shade of red. But on the plus side, it did help instill a pretty solid work ethic. Perhaps that also came from the sport background. I don't think I've ever been particularly talented, but I do know how to grind and get things done. Others might call it being stubborn…

As my senior school years loomed ever closer, I knew that I needed to make a decision. The next step had to be taken, but I had no idea what they should be. Up until that time, it seemed as if everything was on autopilot. There was always a natural progression – year 7 was proceeded by year 8, and so on. I wasn't required to critically think about anything much.

With a little guidance, I eventually decided that a degree in Earth Sciences might be a way to go. I really can't tell you why or how I came to that decision. It may well have been that I saw a friend going for it, and I decided to follow suit.

What I do know is that I soon received an offer to study at Imperial College in London, and after my grades came through, that's where I was headed.

The Lonely Desert

University was a shock to the system. To say I struggled with it would be an understatement. And I realize how facetious that statement seems, and that there are millions (if not billions) of people in the world that would have traded places with me in an instant.

Nonetheless, as a shy, quiet, family boy, I didn't handle the change very well. The move to the big city, the workload, the new people – these things all added up, resulting in a shed load of stress, and even bouts of mild depression. Academically, I always felt a few big steps behind my new peers too. I felt as if I didn't belong, and that something just wasn't right.

As you may have predicted, I found comfort in my training. Martial arts, football, interval training, running, climbing, swimming, gymnastics, Olympic lifting - anything to keep me moving. Anything to distract my anxious mind.

My mantra was to *go hard or go home.* It sounds pretty cool, but it only works for so long.

The hefty combination of mental and emotional stress, the physical toll I was putting on my body, and the nagging feeling that I should be elsewhere – it accumulated to near breaking point.

I'd had minor issues with mouth ulcers since my late teens, but these got a whole load worse at university, sometimes to the point where I would be unable to eat or talk properly. I was also constantly tired and getting digestive issues, along with niggling injuries and back problems. It got to the stage where I was not even able to train regularly, so my only outlet and coping mechanism was now unavailable.

All the warning signs of adrenal fatigue were there, but at the time I was too stubborn to stop and listen to my body.

The low point came in early December 2012, when I received a set of blood test results that suggested the likely possibility of Crohn's disease. Although there was never an official diagnosis, I was faced with the possibility of a lifetime on medication.

That was the big wake up call. Perhaps a little naively, right at that moment I decided that the pills and potions were not for me. I wanted to solve this problem on my own, or at least give it my best shot.

It sounds a little silly, looking back, but I truly believe that it set the wheels in motion for me to forge a different path – ultimately one to a more fulfilling way of life, and the possibility of financial freedom.

From Camel to Lion

German philosopher Friedrich Nietzsche was an interesting character. He's one of the people I stumbled upon during my early investigations into personal development, recommended to me by a good friend.

One of my favorite ideas he put forth was that of the spiritual metamorphosis, and his archetypes of the camel, lion, and child. Nietzsche considered these to be stages of spiritual growth that humans are able to transition through.

Like many others, for a good portion of my life I spent the majority of my time in the camel phase. What does that mean exactly?

I may have interpreted this in entirely the wrong way, but here's my understanding. The camel is said to carry the weight of the world on their shoulders. They're in many ways submissive creatures, living life on other people's terms, and being weighed down in the process. They're reactive, spending a fair amount of time stressing about things that are out of their control. It can be an exhausting existence.

This is how I often felt, without really knowing it. And it was no one's fault – it's just the way things were. I did the work I was supposed to do, trained for certain sports on certain days, went to the university that I was fortunate enough to be accepted to.

But at the same time I was reactive and self pitying. I felt sorry for myself, but did little about it. And I may well have stayed that way had I not gone through the health issues and transformative process at university.

As Nietzsche once said:

"In the loneliest desert a second metamorphosis occurs, the spirit here becomes a lion; it wants to capture freedom and be lord in its own desert".

This is exactly what university symbolized to me. A lonely desert that allowed me to start uncovering the real me.

This lion phase is characterized by rebellion. By forging a new way. By becoming the master of his destiny. Instead of being submissive and trudging along on a predefined path, the lion is proactive. He stands up against the dragon of societal norms and says "I will!" He fights that dragon until he gets where he wants to be.

This is the fire that began to grow inside me during my time in London. I can't remember exactly when, but I know that it happened sometime around that first doctor's visit.

I realized that I didn't want to head down a career path in the Earth Science world. One that might well bring me financial success, but would provide me with no satisfaction. For some people it's exactly what they've always wanted to do. But it wasn't for me. I knew that something related to health and fitness was where I needed to head if I was to really follow my passion, so I started making changes in that direction.

I wasn't quite a brave enough lion to pack in university altogether, and I'm glad that I didn't. But I did complete a Nutrition Diploma alongside my final year. More recently I qualified as a Personal Trainer too, but that's skipping ahead a few years…

Throughout this transition phase, I continued with my insatiable thirst for knowledge relating to training and healthy living. This led to a number of transformations, including adopting a plant based diet, building a regular meditation practice, and altering the way I trained in order to put less stress on my body.

None of the above came easy at first. But when I delved into the habit changing process itself, things became much clearer. I learnt about not just what to do to live a healthy, more meaningful life, but also how to create lasting, sustainable changes.

To this day I still get the occasional flare up with the health issues, and they may never go away entirely. But my relationship with them has improved. I try not to view the symptoms as a burden, but instead as an opportunity to practice mindfulness and learn more about myself.

This whole process of mild rebellion, learning, and growing got me thinking about how I could use my new found knowledge to help others do the same, and gave birth to the idea of forging my own path.

The Birth of Health Room

As graduation loomed, I was at the risk of slipping back into the camel stage a few times. I was still applying for Earth Science related jobs, and even attended a few interviews. But even though I finished with good grades, my heart wasn't in it, and employers could probably tell.

One night near the end of my stay in London, I was struggling to sleep, which was unusual for me. I'd been thinking for months about what I was going to do upon graduating and churning ideas around my head, but sleep typically came easy.

This night, something was different. It sounds corny, but all of a sudden ideas just started coming to me. Inspiration hit, and I poured my heart out onto a side of A4 paper in the early hours of the morning.

Funnily enough, I still have the piece of paper today, and I read over it from time to time. Most of the things I wrote down have in fact come to fruition over the past few years, which goes to show the power of setting your intentions.

So what did I write?

The paper was split into two halves, the top one of which was structured around a three-step process:

Create a blog. It would be centered on nutrition, fitness, and pretty much everything else under the health and personal development umbrella. The blog would be a way for me to learn new things that I was interested in, and via videos and articles, share my ideas with others in order to help them.

Build a following. Once I'd found my voice, the next step was to find people who could benefit from what I was creating. I wrote about how I would build a presence on social media, and develop a list of email subscribers that I could share my ideas with.

Develop products and services. The next step was to monetize my site. This was to be in the form of eBooks, online courses, affiliate products and online personal training and nutrition consultations.

How I was going to put those three steps into action, I had no idea at the time. I didn't have any experience with website design, copywriting, video production, online marketing, or sales. I was a complete novice, starting from scratch.

But what I *did* have was a big reason why and a strong desire to succeed. And as motivational speaker Dr John Demartini said:

"If your why is strong enough, the how's will take care of themselves".

In case you're wondering, the bottom half of the paper was dedicated to coming up with a name for my brand. I jotted down a few different ideas, but the one theme that kept coming back to me was that of the HERO.

As I mentioned earlier, I'd always been fascinated with superheroes. Particularly those that were seemingly ordinary people who suddenly realized their potential to do extraordinary things. I liked the idea that anyone could become the hero of their own story, and this is a key message that I wanted to get across to my future audience.

I also wanted some sort of play on words, or an acronym. Hence the final name: Health Room, and herohealthroom.com.

The Ups and Downs of Building a Blog

Health Room started as a blank installation, initially hosted free with Wordpress.com. I managed to fumble my way through the initial setup, learning on the job about everything from coding to graphic design. It's a prime example of my stubbornness shining through, and my early in ability to ask for help.

In my very first article on the site I talked about how complex the notion of health actually is. How it's made up of many different interacting components. That the whole is greater than the sum of its parts, and that no one (me included) really had the answer. It's another key message I wanted to get across with the site, and one that I try to carry forward today.

I didn't want to put myself across as an expert in anything in particular, and even though I've gained a fair bit of knowledge and experience since starting the business, it's something I'm still mindful of today. I'd rather be known as a self-experimenter and sharer of ideas, as opposed to someone who has all the answers.

And idea sharing was something I did a fair bit of in the early days of the site. It went hand in hand with the mission of recovering from my own health issues. I would read about certain habits or practices that had been studied or proved beneficial to others, test them on myself, and share my thoughts on the blog.

Initially I wrote as much content as I could, putting out 2-3 articles each week. I was having great fun, and learning a lot about myself and the world around me on the way. But there were a couple of issues:

The first was that I had completely forgotten about step 2 of the master plan – building a following.

Like most new bloggers I thought it was all about publishing great content, and then traffic would generate itself. It would go viral, as they say.

The reality was that even though I was sharing some pretty useful, interesting ideas, the only people reading them were my supportive girlfriend, family members, and a handful of people I'd interact with online. I had no email list, no social media following, and no one paying any interest whatsoever in what I was doing.

The second issue was that because of the lack of step 2, step 3 (making a living) was irrelevant.

I wrote an eBook on plant based nutrition and offered online coaching, but had no one to sell those things to.

I was fortunate to have the support of my loved ones during those early times, both financially and emotionally. Some did struggle to understand what it was that I was trying to achieve, but I don't blame them whatsoever. It was hard for me to articulate it at the time, and I didn't know enough to provide them with much confidence.

I hit another stroke of good fortune by receiving a young entrepreneur's bursary from the Welsh government, which helped keep me going. Without it I may well have packed things in and wouldn't be sat here sharing my story today.

But I knew that the bursary (and to some extent, the patience of my loved ones) probably wasn't going to last forever. I had to figure out how to turn this blogging thing that I enjoyed so much into something that was profitable.

From Blog to Business

So began my real journey into learning about building an online business. I sought out the best websites I could find on doing just that – Copyblogger, Backlinko, and Quick Sprout just to name a few.

I soaked up the knowledge from these online experts and applied things as best I could. Some of the major changes I made after the first year of Health Room included:

Switching my website to become self-hosted, which gave me much more control over monetization and the design of the site.

Publishing more in depth content on a less regular basis. I currently put out a big guide every 1-2 months, and I get much *more* traffic and engagement than I did when I was releasing articles 3 times per week.

Optimizing my content not just for people, but for search engines and popular keywords in my industry. This was something I was initially reluctant to do, but it's made a huge difference and allowed me to spread my message to a wider audience.

Reaching out to influential people in my niche after releasing a new piece of content. That's one of the beautiful things about this industry – there's always someone a few rungs up the ladder, and more often than not they're willing to help out and share your content if it's of value to their followers.

Building an email list using content upgrades (eBooks, guides, cheat-sheets etc.) and popups that were custom built for individual blog posts.

Guest blogging on notable sites in my niche. Including Mind Body Green, Natural News, No Meat Athlete, Tiny Buddha, and numerous others. This has helped to drive traffic back to Health Room, and helped with search engine optimization.

There were a million and one other things that I adjusted and tweaked, but not all of them turned out as I hoped. As Pareto's 80-20 principle describes, it's likely that 20 percent of your efforts bring in 80 percent of your results. So the ideas above are my 20 percent – they're the ones that that *really* started to pay dividends, and still do so today.

My 80 percent, or the things that haven't worked too well for me so far include:

Focusing too much effort on social media. Instagram and Twitter work extremely well for some people, but for me the effort to benefit ratio isn't currently worth it. Building my email list and using bookmarking sites like Reddit have proven a much more valuable use of my time.

Monetizing Health Room with ads. I played with Adwords for a little while on my site, and it paid enough to cover my web hosting. But I soon realized that it wasn't the route I wanted to go down long term. It works well for some websites, but for me it just didn't really feel right having a random advert about weight loss pills sitting next to my article where I talked about avoiding fads and quick fixes…

Trying to do everything on my own. Human beings are interactive creatures. We thrive when we work together. My progress would have been much quicker had I been able to drop my ego sooner and ask others for help. This is still something I struggle with from time to time, but I'm improving!

By making mistakes and learning from them, slowly but surely my traffic began to creep up. In a year we went from a few hundred unique visitors a month and no email subscribers, to 30 thousand a day, more than 2 thousand email subscribers, and a number of highly ranked blog posts that continue to bring in organic traffic and potential customers.

I'm well aware that I'm still a small fish in the ocean of online business, and that the stats above are nothing to scoff at. But I've reached a formula that's working for me, which is such an important part of growing. There's no one-size fits all approach. I can now replicate that formula, making a few tweaks here and there as I go, and I truly believe that growth of Health Room will only accelerate.

The great thing about developing a modest following is that it has allowed me to understand what people really want to learn about, and has allowed me to develop products and services targeted to their needs.

I created an online course last year called Healthy Habits 101, which helps people bridge the gap between having an idea, and taking action. It provides you with the framework to develop new healthy habits, and get rid of any old ones that are holding you back. So far we've had more than 3 thousand people sign up and take the course, and the feedback has been overwhelmingly positive.

The course, alongside my HERO Store (where I share a range of health and fitness related affiliate products that I use and believe in) and online fitness and nutrition coaching, have allowed me to monetize my blog in a way that provides maximum value to those that visit.

However, I'd be lying if I said that Health Room alone is currently an enormous enterprise that provides me with complete financial freedom. I'm still not quite there yet, but there is another part of my business that does help keep me going…

The Freelance Game

Guest blogging was initially a way for me to grow my site, but it sparked the idea of getting paid to produce content for others. Wellness companies and brands were bound to be looking for people to help out, and I now had the resume to say that I had been featured on fairly notable sites in my niche. It seemed like a natural progression.

After a little research, I signed up to the freelance platform Upwork, and began working as much as possible alongside my usual Health Room schedule.

I started by writing blog posts, web copy and nutrition plans for a range of small businesses in the wellness niche, but soon realized that the skills I had been developing since starting Health Room were transferable to other areas – from financial planning sites and film production companies, to businesses selling supplements or garage doors.

Initially I worked for little more than a few cups of coffee per hour, but as I gained experience with a wide range of clients, my reputation on the site began to grow, and so did the rewards I received for providing my services.

One thing that I was fortunate enough to realize quite early on during my freelancing journey was the value of listening. Again, we introverts are not always that great at talking, but we have a habit of listening and analyzing. I applied this mind-set to my freelance jobs, really trying my best to understand what the client wanted before we went ahead.

Fast forward a few years to the present day, I'm now included in the Top Rated talent pool on the site, and have been fortunate enough to work alongside a number of high profile companies both in and outside the platform.

As well as the monetary benefits, freelancing has also provided me with the chance to hone my craft. I've been able to develop my skills and figure out what works and what doesn't from a content creation and marketing standpoint, and then take these ideas back to improve the other half of my business, Health Room.

As I stated in the very first paragraph, it feels strange to talk about myself as some kind of success story. But I suppose it goes to show that even if you have no background in writing or formal qualifications in online marketing, there are still plenty of opportunities if you go looking for them.

Never Quite Being 'There'

Building an online business is like a never-ending tunnel. The finish line doesn't ever appear. You've never really made it - there's always something bigger and better to move on to. More projects to complete, more people to reach.

This is something that I've realized over the past few years. I've devised milestones that I wanted to hit and slowly ticked them off one by one. But for almost every milestone that I reach, another one pops up in my head that I can add to the list. It's a constant cycle.

The trick, I've realized, is to take a step back now and again. It's still something I'm working on – I'm definitely no expert at it.

But through my journey I've noticed how easy it is to get caught up in the race of reaching the next rung on the ladder. Living this way, life just passes you by. You're predominantly concerned about the future, and you miss out on the present.

By applying self-reflection from time to time, you get the chance to take things in and really acknowledge your achievements. Not in an egotistical kind of way. It's more akin to the practice of gratitude.

This brings us to Nietzsche's final stage of spiritual transformation: the child.

Being a lion is sometimes necessary to get on the path you want to be on. But similarly to that of the camel, it's not always a pleasant existence. Fighting dragons all day long can become exhausting…

From my understanding, the child phase is about acceptance, gratitude, and non-resistance. The child lives in the present moment, and is open to all possibilities. They see the world with awe and wonder. They play, with intent and with full attention. This is the stage that these days I endeavor to be in as much as possible. I dip in and out of from time to time. We all do.

It's akin to the flow state, where whatever you're doing in that moment feels exactly how it should. There's no mental or physical fog holding you back. You're inspired, creative, and unstoppable – a conduit for ideas from a higher place.

That's why these days I make sure to set time aside to play – be it with ideas for Health Room or in my own movement practice. It's time to just be and go with the flow. Being present and having this childlike mind state is in my opinion on of the keys to happiness, health and success in every area of your life – including business.

The Takeaway Message

The Health Room of today is very different to the Health Room of 3 years ago, and I'm sure it will be just as different 3 years into the future. Constant evolution is the key factor – never stop learning, and never stop growing.

Putting together this chapter has been a surprisingly useful experience for me. Writing everything down has helped me to make a little more sense about my journey so far, what's worked for me, and where I want to head in the future.

Even if it's just one small tidbit of wisdom, I really hope that it's provided you with something of value. And if not, thankfully there are 14 other people in this book who no doubt have a plethora of wisdom you can devour.

To make things a little easier to digest, if I could distil the lessons I've learnt over the past few years down to a few succinct bullet points, they'd look a little something like this:

If you want to follow your passion, but you're not sure what it is that you're passionate about, look back to what you did as a child. Often there are plenty of clues if you look hard enough.

Just because you're expected to head down a certain path or you have the ability or opportunity to do so, doesn't mean it's right for you. Sometimes you need to break the mould, become a lion, and stand up for what you believe in to really unlock your potential and get to where you want to be.

You'll make mistakes on the way, particularly as you first start out. It's inevitable. The trick is to view them as learning experiences, as opposed to failures.

Don't be afraid to ask for help. It's not a sign of weakness. We're interdependent beings, and our best work is done when we work together.

Listen to your potential customers. Figure out what they struggle with and how you can solve their problems. Building a successful business is about the value you can provide to people.

Enjoy the journey, as opposed to always reaching for the next goal. Take time to celebrate your accomplishments, big or small. And be grateful. When you want nothing, the world is yours.

Make time for play. It's during those times that you are uninhibited by the stresses of everyday life that your best ideas will come to you.

In essence, the takeaway message is to follow you passion, embrace mistakes, ask for help, listen to your followers, enjoy the journey, and make time for play.

Paige Burkes

Paige Burkes has 25+ years of experience as a strategic CFO/COO helping rapidly growing companies achieve their goals. In her years of experience, she has come to understand that we need to find more effective ways of achieving our versions of success.

The traditional methodologies are no longer working for us. In fact, they're making us more stressed and less happy by the day. Paige works with companies, entrepreneurs and individuals to find and create their personalized versions of success and happiness.

You can read more of her ideas for increasing your own happiness and success at Simple Mindfulness (www.simplemindfulness.com).

The Winding Road to Happiness

As you grow up, you're programmed to believe that you're supposed to have your whole life figured out by the time you're 21 years old.

Here's the plan:

1. Graduate from high school with good grades so you can
2. Get into college and graduate so you can
3. Get a "good job" where you earn a decent paycheck so you can
4. Attract the perfect mate and get married so you can
5. Have 2.3 kids, a dog, a big house with a big mortgage so you can
6. Live happily ever after.

Has anyone actually done that?

You're fed this story as you grow up and wonder what's wrong with you when life doesn't turn out that way. You think you're letting yourself and others down when everything doesn't play out perfectly. Get over it. Life doesn't work that that. Life is messy and hard and fun and interesting. It's a ride to enjoy, not a mission to accomplish.

If you're feeling the pressure of your family or friends who are asking what your plans are for the rest of your life, ask them if they had it all figured out at 21, 30 or even 40. If they say "yes," they're either lying, or they settled and decided to do what their parents wanted them to do without asking themselves if it was right for them, and they're a little jealous of you doing otherwise.

Here's a more likely story:

1. Struggle to make it through high school so you can
2. Hopefully get into college and maybe graduate so you can
3. Get a low-paying job (if you're lucky) that you hate that has nothing to do with your major so you can
4. Struggle to pay the rent and those giant student loans while you
5. Wonder what's wrong with you and why you don't have your life all figured out which results in
6. Being depressed and anxious which prevents you from
7. Finding a mate which causes you to
8. Experience deeper depression and anxiety and generally feel like a loser.

I'd like to propose a different approach to life – one that you can actually feel good about.

The first scenario is a huge set of expectations that society thrusts upon you without your buy-in. You take it on because you think it's what everyone is supposed to do. The myths in the media, school, religion and everywhere else pump you full of these ideas.

And when you can't live up to these expectations (or you don't want to), you feel bad about it, like there's something wrong with you. If this is you, you are the majority. Only about 1% of the population actually accomplishes the first plan, and most of them aren't happy.

My Story

When I graduated from college over 25 years ago, I thought I had things all figured out.

I actually got as far as step 4 in the first plan before I woke up one day and thought, "Is this really what I want to be doing for the rest of my life?" The clear answer was "No!" but I had no idea what I *did* want.

This is the story of an accountant run amok. A woman who had her life planned out, mapped out, short-term and long-term goals set, thought she knew exactly what she wanted out of life, was on the fast track to success in her career. Then she woke up one morning and said, "What the f**k!" And her life changed forever.

I grew up in New Orleans, made good grades and graduated high school near the top of my class (step 1). I moved to Boston for college where I majored in accounting and graduated cum laude (step 2) and was one of the lucky few who had a job before I graduated (step 3). A couple years out of college I met who I thought was the man of my dreams and got married (step 4).

When the topics of kids and buying a house came up (step 5), I had a block. It wasn't the right time yet. I could feel it in my bones that I couldn't move on to the next step of my life plan.

I worked as a senior manager at a big public accounting firm in Boston. I was on a mission to become a partner faster than anyone else ever had. When it was apparent that I was about a year away from that, this nagging voice in the back of my head started asking, **"Is this all there is to life?"** I started to closely examine the lives of the partners I worked for and hoped to hell that I didn't end up like them. I wanted so much more out of life.

Around that time, I was offered a short-term position as the chief financial officer (CFO) of a company. I thought that maybe working on the inside of a company might be different than auditing one so I accepted. I thought I could always go back to the big firm when this project was over.

Within a couple months, I was miserable and knew that this wasn't "it."

Stepping into the Unknown

Having completed that project, I had made enough of a move physically and emotionally to realize that I couldn't go back to the big firm. *I couldn't accept mediocrity for the rest of my life.* I had no idea where to go or what to do next, but I knew that I couldn't go back. It was just too painful.

This was the beginning of a huge shift in my life: from being incredibly organized and full of plans to someone who learned to go with the flow and trust my intuition. It's like the old analogy: How do you make a thousand-mile car trip in the dark? By seeing the next twenty feet ahead of you.

My husband at the time was a pilot. He was based on the island of Nantucket, off the coast of Massachusetts. Not knowing where to go next, I packed up our apartment in Boston, put everything in storage and moved to Nantucket – in the winter. We lived in a bed and breakfast whose owner let us run it for the pilots who needed an overnight place to stay. I learned about the B&B business and decided that it wasn't something I wanted to do.

I waitressed at one of the two restaurants open on the island in the winter (big jump from corporate big shot). *Never let your ego believe that you're too good or too big for anything.* That job opened many awesome opportunities for which I never could have planned.

The First Big Adventure

One evening after work, I was talking with the other staff. Another waitress said she was going on a trip to Costa Rica in a few weeks, and her friend who was supposed to go with her bailed so she didn't know what to do. I thought, "Costa Rica has always been on my list of places I'd love to visit." So I asked if I could go with her. She was ecstatic to not have to cancel her trip, and I was about to cross something off my bucket list.

We left a few weeks later with our backpacks, a hotel reservation for the night of arrival and our Lonely Planet Guide to Costa Rica (latest edition was 10 years old). It was the most amazing month and a half of my life. *I learned the magic of serendipity and happiness when I let go of plans and stop trying to control things.* The experiences I had and the people I met were so much better than anything I could have planned.

When I returned, I knew I couldn't stay on Nantucket forever but didn't know what to do next. Around that time, my intuition started to scream at me, "Go west and do something with horses." My logical mind replied, "Where west? It's awfully big. And what with horses? There's a lot I could do (even though I had done nothing with horses except some trail rides at camp when I was a kid)." My intuition wisely replied, "You go figure it out." And I did.

People often ask how I could have made such a leap. Until that time, I hadn't thought much about following my intuition. The voice, my intuition, started by whispering to me. The more I didn't listen, the louder it became. Finally, it became so loud that I had to listen to it. I felt that I had no other alternatives. I knew I would never be happy if I didn't take this next step. The pain of staying the same was more than the pain and fear of changing.

When your intuition speaks, LISTEN and ACT on it. It always has your best interest in mind.

I informed my husband at that time that we were leaving in two weeks. He asked, "Where? And do what?" I had always been the one with very clear goals and plans, so he thought I had everything mapped out. I got the "deer in the headlights" from him when I responded that I had no idea, but we just had to go.

Go West Young Woman!
Two weeks later we packed my Jeep and headed west. From Boston we headed straight for Colorado. We explored Colorado, Wyoming, Montana, Idaho, Washington, Oregon and northern California.

My intuition said that "something" would pop up along the way. And if it didn't, we would end up at my brother's place in San Francisco.

We explored some amazing places, but nothing popped up. We landed at my brother's place for a couple weeks where I explored San Francisco and did online research to find something "west and horses."

I discovered an outfitting school outside of Jackson Hole, Wyoming. This is where you live in a tent in the deep woods for a month and a half and learn how to cook over an open fire, pack horses, hunt, fish and be a guide. This is serious outdoor living, and I was intrigued.

Mind you, I was a major city girl who thought, "Ewww! Dirt and bugs!" at the thought of camping up to this point. **But now I was open to anything.** And now I was going to be the female version of Jeremiah Johnson.

I called and registered at the last minute. Upon arrival at the camp, I found that another woman and I were the first women they had ever had at this school which had been running for 25 years.

It was another absolutely amazing experience. I learned levels of self-sufficiency that I never thought I had in me. Going from city girl to this, doing it well and loving it – *I knew I could handle anything that would ever be thrown at me.*

By the end of the school, I knew I didn't want to be an outfitter. I remembered a vacation I took a couple years earlier to a dude ranch in Telluride, Colorado. I remember looking up at the peaks and the amazingly blue sky thinking, "I have to be here. I don't know how or when, but I have to be here." (It's that little voice talking to me again.)

Well, two years later, I was there asking for a job. Funny how the Universe works. They understandably told me to get lost (in a very nice way) since they only knew me as the city slicker guest that I had been.

Next, I called the Colorado Dude Ranchers Association and asked if they knew of anyone hiring. They said that, since it was very late in the hiring season (late May), usually there's nothing available, but they happened to know of a ranch looking for a manager. Perfect! I'm a manager!

I called the owner and talked for a couple hours. He invited us to the ranch where we spent a couple days. At the end of the second day he said, "Well, why don't you stay?" And we did.

I learned the ropes of all the positions at the ranch that summer. Every time I took guests out for a ride I would say (sometimes to myself, but usually to the guests), "I can't believe I get paid to do this. Other people are going to offices and jobs they hate, and I get to be *here*. Amazing!"

As fall turned into winter, the guests disappeared and my already weak marriage fell apart. He wasn't up for this new lifestyle that I was so passionate about. He returned to Boston, and we divorced.

I was alone at the ranch. It was the most peaceful time of my life. Guests that came for a night or two would ask me if I was scared to be there alone. They thought it was like the movie, *The Shining*. I would always laugh and say that I was much more scared in a city than I ever was out in the woods.

During that winter, I met the true man of my dreams. He managed a wildlife center up the road from the ranch I managed. I took guests to his center to see and learn about the wolves, bear, mountain lions, fox, bobcat and other wildlife there. When things were slow at the ranch, I would drive up to his center and help care for the wolves.

After a year at the ranch, I knew it wasn't the "west and horses" that I was looking for, so I moved on. Next I worked at a local university's equine program on the feed crew, caring for a few hundred horses and working with a trainer learning how to start horses.

This was followed by another manager position at a unique horse ranch in California. Neither of these were "it" either, but I continued to learn new things from my different experiences.

Are you getting the picture here? ***Life is a series of experiences that all have meaning.*** In order to know what you want, you have to have a lot of experiences that help you narrow things down. None of them are bad. None of them are failures. Each one helps you to put the pieces together a little better.

And as you put the pieces together, the picture in the puzzle of your life changes. What's good for you and what you want will change over time. It's perfectly normal.

Keep stepping out of your comfort zone and having more amazing experiences.

Settling Down

After a couple years, while I loved the outdoor life, I was tired of taking care of other people's horses at other people's places for minimum wage. I wanted my own place and my own horses. I felt that the only way I could get this would be to return to a corporate job *but to live where and how I wanted.*

Six months later I found a great job. In case you're wondering, my two year "sabbatical" was an asset on my resume and in my job search. I gained many valuable experiences, and most of the people interviewing me were a little jealous that I had taken the leap and done things they only dream of.

With paycheck in hand, my new husband and I went house hunting. It took some searching but we found our dream house on 20 acres in the mountains southwest of Pikes Peak and Colorado Springs. We got our own horses and moved his mountain lions from the wildlife facility he managed to a big enclosure in our back yard. This time, buying a house together felt like the perfect thing to do.

Knowing that I didn't want to make the hour and a half commute every day to my new job, I negotiated with my boss to work from home one day a week. Then I pushed it to two or three days a week.

The days I worked from home, things were flexible. My husband and I would go for long walks each day and spent lots of time together. I made telecommuting flexible and seamless so that, usually, no one knew whether I was in the office or not. Without a commute, I probably worked more hours than if I had been at an office, but the flexibility made it worth it.

Near the end of my eight years with this company, I worked from home full time. I was the VP of Finance of this company with a staff to manage. Many would say that it's impossible to work this kind of job remotely. *I knew it was possible, and I made it happen.*

Since then, I've held other CFO and COO (chief operating officer) roles for companies from startup to $90 million in revenues, public, private and non-profit. In almost every case, I've maintained a flexible schedule, frequently working from home.

We live in the same amazing house with fabulous views, wildlife everywhere and three kids with whom we share our slice of heaven. Although I may be doing some of the same things I used to in other corporate jobs where I wasn't happy, I've learned to find a bigger purpose and live life on my own terms. And that makes all the difference.

With all these experiences, I've learned that I can only be happy working with companies that share my values. While you and your company may share a common mission, if your values aren't aligned, the fit will never be right, and you'll find it difficult to be happy there.

Sharing My Lessons to Help Others

In 2010, I started my blog (www.simplemindfulness.com) to help others see the possibilities for great things in their lives. The writing process over the years has been eye-opening for me. Early on, I learned how much of myself I was still hiding behind the corporate persona that I wore so well. I learned how much more effectively I can connect with and help others by dropping all the personas, being myself and telling my stories.

Many people think they could never do many of the things I've done. I didn't think I could do them either – until I did them. Leaving a successful career. Making major leaps out of my comfort zone multiple times (something I HIGHLY recommend). Creating my own lifestyle. People may question why I wanted to do many of the things I did. I say, why not?

I remember a phone call with my mother when I was at the dude ranch. She asked, "Don't you think you're being a bit irresponsible?" I thought that was the most bizarre question. I answered, "Absolutely not!" I thought I was doing the most responsible thing ever – making the journey to find myself and my passions and live life to the fullest. It's the only way I could be happy.

Life Is an Experiment

Look at your entire life as an opportunity to experiment. Don't stop experimenting at any age because you think it's too late or you're too old to change. It's never too late.

With each new experience, learn something about yourself. Notice what you're drawn to and what you don't like. With your next experiment, do more of what you're drawn to. There's no such thing as "failure" if you're experimenting. You're always learning.

If you're not sure what to do next, just do something – anything. Action brings learning and more actions. It doesn't matter which direction you choose.

When I left my first corporate job, I followed my intuition that simply said, "Go west and do something with horses." I had no idea what that meant, but I started by doing something – anything – that fit that description. I tried lots of things. Some worked. Some didn't. I learned an immense amount about myself in the process.

Whatever you choose to do, make sure it's something that feels right *for you* and pushes you a little out of your comfort zone. Don't worry about making other people happy. It's your job to live your own life and make yourself happy. Don't let anyone guilt you into something different.

You don't have to have anything figured out. There's no race or finish line. We're on this earth for a very limited time. Experiment to discover your unique gifts and find ways of sharing them with the world. That's your only job.

Drop any expectations that you may have or that you think others have of you. Unmet expectations are the source of negative emotions.

While you've been programmed to think that you have to use that college degree, that's not necessarily the case. What makes your heart sing? How would you love to spend your days? The way the world works now, you can probably find a way to make money doing those things, no matter how crazy they seem.

A quick Google search can reveal others who are already doing what you dream of. Reach out and connect with those people. They're waiting for you to ask them how they did it. They want to help you, especially when you can find unique ways to help them.

Being "successful" doesn't mean having lots of money, a "good job," a big house or anything like that. Those are all stories that our culture perpetuates yet have been proven to be false. Success means, first and foremost, loving and accepting yourself just as you are right now. Success means loving what you do and using the gifts that you were born with to help others. Success means simply being happy.

Moving from where you are to a better place won't happen overnight. It won't happen until you decide to make changes. Take baby steps each day toward how you want your life to be (do you know how you want it to be?). Experiment. Some days will be better than others. Keep taking consistent baby steps in a direction you choose and allow your happiness to grow.

I have spent over 25 years as a financial executive. After my first seven years in Corporate America, I wondered if that was what I was supposed to do with the rest of my life. The intuitive answer was a resounding "no" but I didn't know what the answer was. Later, I discovered that this "no" was more about my lifestyle (programmed by society and family) and less about my job.

Through my years of experiences and experiments, I've found that I enjoy helping companies achieve their versions of success. At my jobs, I also enjoy helping the people I work with overcome their issues and find their happiness. I continue my work online to reach more people and inspire them to mindfully, intentionally create better lives for themselves.

With all that I've been through, I know that **anything is possible if you want it badly enough**.

This is why my passion is to support and work with as many people as possible to guide them along their path to living their own version of the good life.

Simple Steps to Create Your Own Amazing Life:

Help other people

If you're struggling to figure out what to do with the rest of your life, my initial suggestion is to stop focusing on yourself and all that's wrong. Find people who you can help.

What are you good at that you take for granted? What are things that others compliment you on that you think are "no big deal." Those are your gifts. Find ways to share them.

Using myself as an example, some of my skills are in finances and being analytical yet I love being around creative types (who are usually not the best at finances and analytical thinking). I found an organization that matched people like me with artists who needed help managing their finances. I loved the challenge and loved using my gifts to help people. The artists loved and appreciated not only my helping them with their businesses but also that I understood them as people. I understood and respected how they think.

Find your happiness

My next suggestion would be to find the happiness that's buried inside you. Let it out. Don't tell yourself that you can't be happy until the stars align and everything falls perfectly into place. Even if that happened, the happiness would be fleeting.

Being happy is a decision. It doesn't matter what your situation is. In every moment, you're choosing how you feel. Practice mindfulness by taking a deep breath and noticing how you feel in the moment. Do you want to feel that way? If not, make a new choice.

Let go of expectations

Feeling like you've let others down is a story you tell yourself. I'm guessing that it's probably not working very well for you. How about making up a new story that creates more positive feelings in your heart?

If others are telling you that you've let them down, ask yourself if you happily agreed to live up to their expectations. Trying to live up to others' expectations is impossible. It's the sure-fire path to unhappiness.

You can't make other people happy. That's their job. Your job is to make you happy and that comes from inside. If you say, "I'll be happy when…." then you'll never be happy. Smile a big smile right now and hold it for at least 30 seconds, even if (especially if) you don't feel like it. Do that a few times a day. You'll be surprised how effective it can be in turning around your mood.

Express your gratitude

Find things to be grateful for throughout your day and write them down. Carry a journal or write them in your phone somewhere. Things you can be grateful for now:

You have people in your life who love you;

You're free to change jobs;

You're alive and healthy;

You're free to start over and make new choices whenever you want;

You have eyes with which you can see the sky, clouds, flowers and the people around you;

You have food, clean water and clothes.

Whenever I look at a flower or anything beautiful, I say "thank you" for the opportunity to experience that little bit of beauty.

If you're grateful for something about another person, by all means, let them know. Do not assume that they already know. You'll make their day.

Experiment

Whether you're at a job you hate, a job you put up with or (lucky you) while you're not working and have plenty of time on your hands, experiment a little every day. Journal your innermost thoughts. Take classes that interest you, not ones you think will lead to a job. You never know where those classes, your experiences, the people you meet and the things you learn will take you.

Life is most definitely a journey of up's and down's, high's and low's. Every experience is an opportunity to learn more about yourself and make new choices. It's up to you to take responsibility for your own life. No one is a victim unless they choose that path (which I wouldn't recommend if you want to be happy). Take the first step toward your dream today. If you don't, when will you? What's worse: tip-toeing outside of your comfort zone today to create a new life for yourself, or having your life be exactly as it is now five, ten or twenty years from now? Every moment you have the opportunity to make a new choice.

Rob Cubbon

I am a slacker who turned into an entrepreneur.

I haven't a clue what's going on but I seem to be able to do this business thing. I used to work for other people but now I experience life as an entrepreneur – travelling the world and doing what I want. For me, life is better when you do what you want.

I'm an Amazon bestselling author, online teacher, graphic designer and ex-slacker who wants freedom for you and success for your business.

In 2006 I was wasting my life away on a string of mundane jobs in offices. Since 2008 I've been working from home earning money doing what I love (robcubbon.com). And now *I'm travelling the world.*

How to Get Laid

I would love to tell you that I'd meant to do this.

It would be great to say that I woke up one morning pissed with my boss, walked into my stressful, high-end job and gave him the finger.

That's not what happened. What happened to me was *ten times better than that*.

I was never entrepreneurial. As a kid, I never sold lemonade outside my parent's house on sunny days. That's not the sort of thing English people do and, besides, you don't get many sunny days there either.

My best plan was to join a band, become successful and live a better, sexier life happily ever after.

Unfortunately, my role models for this plan were the Beatles and the Rolling Stones. So as I hadn't struck worldwide success and fame by age 22, I had to give up on that idea.

Damn, I'm not going to be a rock star so I'm going to be working in a job for the rest of my life.
I didn't have a Plan B.

So Plan A, Part I: Get a job in an interesting industry

I ended up getting a job for a magazine.

I hated that job. I'm not sure if I was expecting to enjoy it or not. I didn't. It was monotonous work and a lot of meaningless office politics.

Plan A, Part II: Leave my depressingly boring job

I then freelanced for magazines and newspapers so I at least wouldn't be working at the same place all the time and, with any luck, I could work a little less as well.

This didn't work.

The work was still endlessly boring. The hours were still long. It was going to be decades before I would get the experience necessary to do creative work. And, I looked at those in their 40s, 50s and 60s who had those "better" jobs. They were over-weight, bitter, bullying, bad-tempered souls who didn't look happy.

I didn't want to end up like them

And the people of my own age seemed better than me at everything. Better at doing the job. Better at getting on with people at work. Better at relationships outside work. Better at enjoying work. Or maybe they just were better at hiding the despair we all feel.

One of the many freelance jobs I had at the time was a night shift at a newspaper's picture desk. Nothing much happens on newspaper's picture desk between the hours of 9pm and 1am. And, to deal with the boredom, I spend hours playing around with Adobe's image editing software, Photoshop.

I quite enjoyed messing around with computers. Since I didn't like working with people, I thought I'd work with computers instead.

So, in my endless quest to make my life more comfortable, I hit on another plan.

Plan A Part III: Get graphics software freelance work

This was five years in to my working life. I was to spend the next 15 years freelancing with graphics software. Trudging round to different office blocks in London.

For so long, I was unhappy.

It was as if I was sleep-walking. The months and years rolled past – I was unable to distinguish between them. One job was much like another.

I was almost out of ideas.

The work was undemanding and boring. I was working with people who I didn't understand. I never got to know any of my colleagues because I was never long at any job.

Plan A Part IV: Continue freelancing but drink a lot, take drugs and hit on girls to relieve the boredom.

I crammed onto underground trains at Finsbury Park every morning and along with millions of other people going to work in central London.

I didn't have any ambition or aspiration other than to make my life as comfortable as possible and to have a good time.

This involved getting drunk with my friends, smoking marijuana, watching TV, and hitting on girls.

When I got home from work in the evening, I'd roll a large marijuana joint and turn on the TV. Weed, beer and soap operas were my constant companions.

During the weekends, I'd drink more, smoke more, take Class A drugs (ecstasy and cocaine), and try to chat up women. Unsuccessfully.

Lack of motivation, cigarette smoking, over indulgence in alcohol and drugs, bad diet, lack of exercise, and, above all, negative thinking, all took their toll.

I experienced many, many dark times. I was depressed.

There was no Plan B. I continued like this. For. Ten. Years.

The breakthrough

Something I did one day, when I was browsing the Internet hoping no one would see what I was typing, changed everything

One day, I entered some words into a search engine that would change my life.

The words I typed in were: *how to get laid.*

I ended up on a site by Ross Jeffries called something like SpeedSeduction.net.

Arriving at this website changed my life (but not in the way you think).

There were two thoughts that flashed through my mind:

This guy must be making a shit ton of money

And, I wonder if this works

The seduction website made several references to neuro-linguistic programming (NLP). So NLP became my next port of call.

I never bought Ross Jeffries's product. But it piqued my interest and set me on a path of learning, reading, researching, and discovering that eventually led me to a better place.

Meditation

I borrowed books from the library and read as much as I could on the subject. A lot of NLP techniques involved sitting with your eyes closed and trying to calm your mind. Many NLP books advocated meditation.

So I pulled up a chair, got comfortable, closed my eyes, and turned my attention to my present experience, vaguely trying to concentrate on my breathing or to work through some NLP technique.

For the first time in my life, I was feeling in control.

I no longer felt as though life happened to me. I felt that I could change my life from the inside, instead of being changed by external events. I had tools to help me now. I felt empowered.

So I read. And I read, and I read, and I read. Amazon wish lists and its *people-who-bought-this-also-bought-that* recommendations became my friends.

NLP led me to books about meditation; books about meditation led me to books about Buddhism. Before long, I was reading about Taoism, Hinduism, Kabbala, mysticism, Reiki, psychology, self help, personal development, spirituality, and so on.

Every day, along with reading books, I meditated.

There are many different ways to meditate. The method I've settled on for the last 15 years is concentrating on the breath.

Meditation is the non-judgmental experience of the present moment. The object of meditation is to quiet the thoughts.

Our minds think constantly throughout the day, and it's seemingly impossible to turn these thoughts off. The more I watched my thoughts, the more unnecessary this mental chatter seemed to be. And I could see how damaging my habitual thinking and beliefs had become.

So now I was watching my thoughts and trying to keep them positive and less judgmental.

You can change your thoughts, your character, and even your immediate environment from the inside out

I was intrigued by the Buddhist concept of *right thought*. *Right speech* and *right action* I could understand: you should not hurt others with words or deeds. But I'd previously been unaware of how wrong thoughts could be hurtful—and mostly hurtful to the thinker.

The combination of meditation and watching my thoughts stopped some negative thought patterns and beliefs. At the age of thirty-three this was life changing.

Within a few days of practicing five to ten minutes of daily meditation, my dark moods stopped.

As my dark moods lightened, so did my personality. I smiled and had more time for people, and consequently they smiled back and had more time for me.

But another thing happened that was truly life changing.

Clearing the smoke

I had been a cigarette smoker since the age of eighteen—a habit I truly detested. My clothes smelled, my breath smelled, I smelled.

I'd resigned myself to a life of cigarette smoking and thought that giving up smoking was just another achievement that was beyond me—along with having a girlfriend or any meaning in my life.

I found meditation made me feel clean in a way. I remember feeling this clean feeling first thing in the morning. After making my coffee and toast, I habitually looked at the half-full pack of cigarettes discarded from the night before.

"Oh god," I said to myself. "I really don't want to put one of those in my mouth now." I'd just cleaned my teeth; why would I light that foul-tasting thing and suck the noxious smoke into my nice clean lungs?

If you've never smoked you'd probably think this was an obvious concern. But, as a smoker, you love the first cigarette in the morning. And the hunger for cigarettes doesn't leave you until last thing before you go to bed. And so it continues the next day.

However, on this particular day, this hunger wasn't with me.

"That's strange," I said to myself. It was more than just strange; it was out of this world. This addiction had been with me for well over fifteen years.

All this flashed through my mind as I looked at the half-full pack of cigarettes that morning.

I was fully expecting to get the urge to smoke at some point during the day. However, I thought I'd go about my normal business and see what happened.

At the end of the day, I sat and looked at the pack of cigarettes. Now, this pack of cigarettes had no more hold over me than any of the other objects on my table.

The next morning, after my coffee and toast, I glanced down at the pack and again felt no compulsion to smoke. I was indeed cured.

Days passed. Weeks passed. I never smoked again. I left the pack there as a reminder. Finally, I threw it away.

Lifting the head fog

Marijuana affects different people in different ways. Many of my friends maintain that they work better whilst smoking it.

Personally speaking, weed demotivates me, harms my short-term memory and, generally, forces me in on myself.

However, as I'd giving up smoking nicotine, I'd also stopped smoking weed. At the same time I'd increased my exercise routines, ate better food, started to drink less and stopped taking other drugs.

My memory, cognition, and creativity all improved within days of starting meditation and stopping smoking weed.

Suddenly, I regained the childlike enthusiasm and interest in the world that had been beaten out of me by school and work-life.

Website

I was spending a lot of time online researching and discovering. I'd always wanted to create a website for myself but had decided that HTML and web publishing was beyond me.

Now, with greater confidence in my mental abilities, I set out to create a static three-page portfolio website with some examples of graphics work that I'd done.

Graphics were no problem as I'd been using Photoshop for years. Even so, it took me months and months but, finally, in 2005, I managed to create a three-page static site with HTML at RobCubbon.com.

I was so pleased with myself that I was even talking to some people at work about it.

I was incredibly lucky that someone recommended WordPress.

Getting clients

I carried on going from freelance gig to freelance gig, and if anyone asked for my details, I had my RobCubbon.com portfolio site with attached blog.

However, questions remained in the back of my mind: *What if I worked for clients directly? How do I get people to come to my site so they can get me to do work for them?*

At home I had Adobe software on my Mac which meant I could do the work I was doing at freelance gigs at home.

Summer 2006, I had a light-bulb moment. A Google search turned up an article that advocated creating more pages to attract traffic to a website.

By this point I could see that my blog, which contained no more than a handful of rubbish posts, was receiving more traffic than the static HTML pages of my portfolio.

The penny dropped. I needed to write more blog posts.

This moment, in 2006, was transformative in my journey of becoming an entrepreneur.

I was somewhat addicted to seeing how many people would come to read my pages: how many, how long for, and what they'd actually typed into Google before arriving at my site. I found this information fascinating.

I do the same thing today: I always check my stats from the previous day: how many visitors; where they've come from; the engagement I've received; how much my products are selling; etc.

As the weeks and months passed, I wrote more, and more visitors came to the site.

At the end of the year three people had contacted me through the website to see if I'd work with them. Suddenly, proper companies were asking me to work with them. This blew me away.

Falling in love with my business

I was stoked, but it was with some trepidation that I ventured into the City of London, where I had been invited to meet with a couple of executives from Accenture. Accenture is a Fortune 500 company with over a hundred thousand employees worldwide. I was absolutely amazed that they'd read my blog and wanted to work with me.

I'm still working with Accenture today. Over the years, that one visit to my website from an Accenture executive has meant hundreds of thousands of dollars profit for my company.

I continued writing more blog posts – longer articles that were better illustrated with images and video. The visitor numbers were increasing.

However, my work day still consisted of bus and underground train journeys I didn't want to be on, turning up late to offices I didn't want to be at, and working alongside people I didn't want to be with.

But, I got more and more work to do from home.

And the quality of work I got through my site was vastly superior to my freelance gigs.

Sometimes I felt totally out of my depth. I must have made a few rookie errors, but somehow I made it through the first few years.

My overall design skills improved.

I was being asked to do projects that were completely different from what I was doing in my freelance gigs. I was learning to say: "yes, I can do that," then trying to figure out how after putting the phone down.

Soon I was being asked to do website designs and other online work.

Simultaneously, I was working to improve my website, getting it to look better by amending various WordPress themes.

My confidence in my abilities improved to such an extent that I gave up doing the freelance gigs and worked on my business from home 100% of the time.

It had taken 2 years from when I got my first client online until I left employment.

It felt great.

Passive income – the beginnings

Also during this time I began to read more business literature. One book that made a great impression on me was *The 4-Hour Workweek* by Tim Ferriss.

I also forced myself to meet other people who shared an interest in online business through London meetups.

I began following bloggers. I was inspired by Tim Ferriss, Glen Allsopp, Lisa Irby, and others (the list is truly endless). I also fell in love with the concept of passive income.

A lot of Internet marketers, John Chow for example, were always saying "the money's in the list" so I started collecting email addresses from my site.

I added a few affiliate links of certain products that I'd mentioned in my blog posts. I also started a YouTube channel and made tiny amounts of money from Google Adsense there and on my site.

I was following ProBlogger, and in one interview Darren Rowse talked to a guy called Pat Flynn who had just started a new blog called SmartPassiveIncome.com.

In the interview Pat Flynn said he'd created an e-book of mostly old blog posts and sold it in the $20–30 range. I couldn't believe this was true, but I thought I might as well try it out myself.

So I created a couple of PDF e-books and sold them to my fledgling list and made a few hundred dollars.

In homage to Pat Flynn, I started publishing a quarterly passive income reports (robcubbon.com/income-reports).

The numbers were modest at first: a few hundred dollars passive income every month.
But I was happy.

I was meditating. I was trying to enjoy the present moment. As I do now. It was still great to be working for my own clients from home. It was bringing in money. Not a fortune but, who cares? It was the same money as I was making in those horrible freelance jobs downtown.

Passive income upturn

Another bit of luck: one of my many blogging contacts, Tara Roskell, mentioned that she'd been selling video courses on an online learning platform called Udemy.

I had a look at the site and decided to bundle together a few of my YouTube videos as a free course.

I was delighted that the course began filling up with students. Pretty soon I was getting positive feedback from people who appreciated my way of explaining WordPress.

I then made a longer, better quality video course showing how to build a great-looking WordPress website from scratch and put this new course up for sale on Udemy.

I made nearly $300 in the first month and nearly $1000 the next month.

I realized the opportunity. So I continued to create more free and paid courses.

I made over $8000 on Udemy in 2013. Over $37,000 in 2014. Over $50,000 in 2015.

During this time, other passive income sources were growing and others were coming into play.

I'd started writing Kindle books. I had a little bit of advertising revenue coming in from Adsense. There were affiliate commissions. And, I was also selling my Udemy courses on a variety of other platforms: Skillfeed (now defunct), Skillshare, StackSocial, Dealfuel, as well as on my own site.

I recorded all this in my income reports (robcubbon.com/income-reports). In 2015, I'd totalled $80,223.13 passive income. And this was on top of what I was earning from my web and graphic design clients.

Leaving London

My marriage had broken down by the end of 2011, five years after our wedding. (I'm writing another book about that now so I'll spare you the details). By September 2014, we had finalized the divorce and sold the house.

By this point, I'd been living in London, England, for 25 years. Every income stream I earned was location independent. I had little reason to live in one of the world's most expensive cities. All I needed was my laptop and decent wifi and I could make a living.

I eventually settled in Chiang Mai, a small provincial town in the north of Thailand. This small city is famously laid back. It also boasts good Internet connectivity, beautiful countryside, friendly locals, as well as a community of business people who work online.

In the last two years I've lived and worked in Chiang Mai, Koh Samui, Koh Phangan, Phuket, Bangkok, all in Thailand; Phnom Penh in Cambodia; Ho Chi Minh City in Vietnam; Cebu in the Philippines; Prague in the Czech Republic; Berlin in Germany; Bratislava in Slovakia; as well as returning to England from time to time.

Two of my greatest loves in my life are travelling and helping people realize their dreams. I'm lucky that I'm able to do these two things most of the time.

I now have more friends in Chiang Mai than anywhere else, although I have no idea where this journey will end.

Where did it all go right?

I trace it all back to that day when I surreptitiously Googled "how to get laid".

That set me on a path of personal development and self-discovery that still isn't over.

I still monitor my thoughts and try to stop them if I think they'll lead to suffering. I still meditate every day.

I still make sure I'm enjoying the moment rather than putting all my attention on a future event. Online business is all about goals. Goals are important but never more important than the present moment.

I'm sure I've benefited from this outlook as I meet a lot of guys in Chiang Mai who aren't happy because they're not as "successful" as they want.

I want to shake them and say, "Dude, you're living in Thailand, you're working for yourself online, you've got a beautiful girlfriend, you have a roof over your head, and can afford excellent food and drink. That's fucking SUCCESS!"

The temptation is to always want more and not appreciate what we have.

We all love the story of someone who's made a fortune overnight. But, why? The faster they've made it the more likely they are to lose it, as far as I've seen.

It's better to figure out a way of making money consistently and build from there.

People say business is difficult and you've got to work, work, work. OK, I've worked hard but not as hard as most and my "success" has not been down to some clever idea.

I've grown my business from nothing. I never put any money into it. I just started working for clients from home and it grew from there.

I didn't suddenly quit my job. I slowly cut down my freelancing in offices bit by bit, until I was sure I could go it alone.

There are no secrets to business success. It's pretty simple but people like to complicate it.

Look at my journey: slow growth through multiple income streams on the back of a personal brand that people trust because of the quality and integrity of the content I've put out. It's not difficult.

It's now a six-figure business. That's not staggeringly successful but it's not bad for a guy that was universally considered an idiot at school and in the jobs he did for 20 years.

I'll never be interviewed on popular entrepreneurial podcasts but this is the model that works for me.

And, most importantly, I'm happy.

I travel the world; I create video courses; I write books; I put out free content; I employ people to help me with some of the tasks I don't like doing; I also employ people to do design jobs for my clients; I have revenue in my business that I'm investing in new brands and new businesses.

Heck, I'm enjoying talking to you right now.

And I'm helping people. I'm inspiring people to discover the amazing life changes that I've benefited from.

Every day, people take one of my free courses at robcubbon.com/freecourses. Every day, I get emails and messages from people saying that I've helped them.

It's amazing to think that at any moment, someone, somewhere in the world, is trying to improve themselves with my content.

Who wouldn't be happy about that?

Steve Mueller

Steve is the founder of **Planet of Success** *(www.planetofsuccess.com/blog), a great choice when it comes to motivation, self-growth and empowerment. This world does not need followers. What it needs is people who stand in their own sovereignty. Join us in the quest to live life to the fullest!*

True Financial Freedom: It's NOT About Money

Most people struggle greatly to attain financial independence because they are confronted with major obstacles on their path towards financial freedom. In most cases, true progress can only be made by identifying these illusions and misconceptions about financial freedom.

Most people will never achieve true financial freedom in their lifetime. This may sound like a blatantly harsh statement at first, but it is the uncomfortable truth nobody wants to talk about. When it comes to financial independence, the majority of people are confronted with major misconceptions and false beliefs that almost make it impossible for them to become financially free. What is worse, these illusions about financial freedom are so dangerous that they prevent people from being financially free – even if they earn six or seven figures a year. It's almost as if these false ideas about money management are ingrained in people from the time they grow up, causing them to do the best they can to never even come close to anything that could be considered as financial freedom.

Mind you, this chapter is not intended as some kind of ridicule of the poor money management numerous people apply in their lives and their false beliefs about being financially free. In fact, I myself struggled with these illusions about financial independence for years. However, I think it's quite important to address the most daunting issues that prevent people from ever attaining the financial freedom they so desire. Consider the following as a guide that helps you to remove major obstacles on your road to financial independence. And perhaps, it may even introduce you to new ways of thinking in regards to the strategies that help you to attain financial freedom.

Throughout my life, I was confronted with major misconceptions and false beliefs that prohibited me from ever coming closer to reaching true financial freedom. Instead of getting closer to my goals, I was chasing mere illusions. Needless to say, I wasted many years during this initial struggle. Luckily, however, being confronted with the tiring effects of the misconceptions about financial freedom forced me to have a closer look at what it was that kept me from making any progress. At the same time, by experiencing these misconceptions about financial independence firsthand, I gradually began to see things more clearly. And once I was able to understand the true nature of the factors that kept me from being financially independent, I was finally able to accelerate my journey towards becoming financially free.

You may be wondering what these illusions about financial freedom are. Let's have a look at them in the following. These were the major obstacles that prohibited me from making any progress in my journey towards financial freedom.

The very first misconception people are confronted with is the belief that financial freedom requires them to earn massive amounts of money. When I began my journey on the long and winding road to financial freedom, I imagined that the only way I could ever reach a certain level of financial independence would be by working myself towards a high figure income. I thought that unless I win the lottery, attaining financial freedom would be almost impossible for me or any other a regular person with an average salary.

However, I forgot (just as the vast majority of people) that earning a lot of money does not necessarily make a person financially independent. Throughout the course of the years, I began to understand that many high earners are also high spenders, which led me to conclude that these people were not at all financially independent, even though they earned significant amounts of money. Certainly, these people portrayed a high level of wealth by all the possessions they accumulated, but they never managed to acquire true independence from the next paycheck. Instead, they used a great proportion of their income in order to finance their expensive lifestyle. To me, owning a lot of material possessions but always having to depend on one's income to continue such a lifestyle does not equal financial freedom. Living such a life is more like having the freedom to fulfill all ones (material) desires that money can buy. However, it is not a life that is truly independent in a financial way.

Whenever I talk to people about financial independence, I always ask them how much money they think they need in order to be financially free. Usually, I hear figures around $3-$5 million, sometimes more, sometimes less. So I also ask them what they intend to do with all that money. And here is where it gets really interesting. Not all but most of them tell me that they are dreaming of an expensive house, multiple sports cars, and various other fancy and costly gadgets. Interestingly enough, not many consider using all this accumulated money in order to generate passive income, which could help them to easily sustain their present lifestyle.

Basically, they dream of becoming multimillionaires in order to lead the supposed lifestyle of a rich person and to experience all the benefits that come with it. In short, they don't necessarily dream of financial independence, they dream of having enough money to afford a luxurious lifestyle. So they don't dream that much of freedom, they dream about boundless consumption. With this dream comes the hope that they can improve their lifestyle notably so that they can live a more luxurious life.

What most do not consider, however, is that once they have a huge villa, they also need suitable furniture for the entire house. They need someone to take care of the house (and the swimming pool of course). Not to mention that their property tax increases (astronomically) as well. And before they even notice, the $3 to $5 million they had in their bank account are spent, leaving them with respectable possessions but no financial independence. However, many of these shiny possessions (such as cars) quickly depreciate in value, which further reduces the net worth of the person. Even worse, they may be putting a lot of pressure onto themselves as it's not that easy (and cheap) to sustain such a lifestyle. In short, instead of being able to leave the financial rat race once and for all behind, they become even more involved in it.

These insights helped me to understand that a great number of people prefer to acquire fancy possessions instead of using their resources to attain financial freedom. Even if they did reach a high income, people with the tendency to prefer material possessions over making good use of their money will not come closer to financial independence. It also showed me that a great number of people think they are financially free just because they can afford to live a luxurious lifestyle. Nothing could be further from the truth. They mistakenly associate their ability to spend significant amounts of money with financial freedom when in actuality they more often than not have to make great sacrifices to earn the money that is necessary for such a lifestyle. These are the people that spend almost all of their money for impressive houses, fancy cars, and various other expensive gadgets. At the same time, none of them is truly financially independent. Instead, their high consumption lifestyle causes them to almost live from paycheck to paycheck (on a sophisticated level). It's almost as if they are stuck in a never-ending absurdity. The more they earn, the more excessively they spend, which ultimately makes them even less financially free. But what happens to this kind of lifestyle when the money begins drying out? It all breaks down like a house of cards. Sustaining an expensive and consumption-driven lifestyle is not at all easy, but it gets even more difficult once a person's income starts to decline or breaks away from one day to the other. The above holds especially true when someone has become used to spend excessively, which makes it even more difficult to cut expenses down once the income begins to decline.

Unfortunately, people mistakenly believe that they are financially free when they are able to afford expensive possessions. Most often, quite the contrary is the case. The more things they acquire, the less independent they become financially. For this reason, problems start to arise as soon as these people are no longer able to generate a high income. While it is exceptionally difficult for regular people to imagine how wealthy multimillionaires can ever become bankrupt, it happens quite often. Marvin Gaye (net worth of $5 million), Dennis Rodman (earned more than $29 million), MC Hammer (net worth of $33 million), Curt Schilling (net worth of $50 million), Francis Ford Coppola (net worth of $52 million), Nicolas Cage (earned more than $150 million), and Mike Tyson (earned $400 million) are only a few examples of people who earned huge amounts of money but also spent it all to the last penny, without using these resources to become financially free. All these people imagined that they are financially free and acted like it, but they did not take the necessary measures in order to ensure that this freedom could be sustained in the future. These examples also highlight that it may be exceptionally difficult to reach financial independence when a person's desires for material possessions know no limits.

What have we learned so far? Well, we've seen that you can earn as much as you want but you will never accomplish financial freedom when you seek to spend almost all of it in order to sustain an expensive and luxurious lifestyle.

During this stage of my journey, I began to realize that ordinary people with an ordinary salary would have to decide whether they wanted to become financially free or if they preferred owning expensive material possessions. It's a tough decision to meet but it's also a necessary one because financial freedom and spending without limits seldom go hand-in-hand – especially if you are earning a regular income. Don't get me wrong: it's perfectly fine if people choose to spend a great deal of their income for whatever they please to own or want to experience. However, it's also necessary to understand that this approach makes it almost impossible to attain financial independence.

It was also a stage of my journey when I began to realize that financial freedom was of a far greater importance to me than living a consumption-driven lifestyle. For this reason, I met the decision to subordinate everything else to my primary goal of attaining financial independence. I began cutting my spending significantly throughout these years. Doing so allowed me to save and invest a lot more money than before. At the same time, my decision enabled me to invest a lot more money annually than many of those who earned a lot more than me but lavishly spent almost all of it. Certainly, there were downfalls to it, but overall, I never regretted my decision to lead a simplistic lifestyle. Quite the contrary, it helped me to avoid accumulating unnecessary and expensive dross that did not contribute any value to my life and to my goal of being financially free.

I am aware that this is quite a radical choice to meet. At the same time, I felt it was a necessary choice in order to increase my chances of becoming financially free.

To most people, living a simple life seems like a boring or even self-restrictive choice. But to me, it is liberating because it has gradually helped me to be happier with less. And once I was pretty comfortable with owning less, I had a lot more financial resources that I could funnel into my primary goal (financial freedom). At the same time, by freeing myself from the tight grasp of materialism, my goal of being financially free started to become a lot more realistic. That's because I no longer desired to own expensive possessions, which ultimately would make it a lot more difficult for me to ever come close to financial independence. Instead, I became perfectly comfortable with living well within my means.

The second misconception is that people believe being financially independent means they can spend without limits. As was already addressed in the above, it does not matter how much money you earn – if you're not in control of your desires and the almost unlimited spending that comes with it, you will most likely not be able to become financially free. At this stage of my journey, I slowly began to understand that people who are financially independent may not necessarily be those who spend lavishly a great proportion of their annual income. Making this realization took me quite some time and it proved to be a challenging obstacle that I had to overcome on my journey to financial freedom. Throughout the course of many years, it helped me to refine my ability to differentiate between people who spend almost all their income in order to portray the lifestyle of a wealthy person and those who were actually financially independent. Doing so allowed me to figuratively separate the wheat from the chaff so that I was much better at identifying people who were truly financially free and those who only portrayed it. It also helped me to learn from the former group while simultaneously ignoring the money management practices of the latter group.

The really interesting thing I began to notice about people who've had accomplished a certain level of financial freedom was that they were exceptionally disciplined consumers who did not only save a great proportion of their income but also limited their spending. They were not necessarily portraying their wealth (or at least their financial freedom) by accumulating expensive possessions. Instead, they invested their money so that it would generate them a passive income, which would allow them to become less and less dependent on their regular income as employees, entrepreneurs or business owners. Over time, doing so helped these financially free people to cover all their expenses from their passive income, which even further accelerated their financial freedom. So instead of having the latest technological gadgets, the fastest car or the biggest house, these people chose to use their financial resources in order to generate a passive income which allowed them to earn more without having to work for it. Isn't that an immensely important aspect of being financially free? To me, it is.

It began to dawn on me that these financially free people were willing to make certain sacrifices in the past (and perhaps still do) in order to reach the financial independence they were looking for. Personally, I think going through this stage can be quite tough. Even more so, I believe that this may be the stage where many people quit, simply because they are pressured into competing with the people around them that spend a lot more money for the acquisition of material possessions. The reason for this is simple: it's really not easy to see all the people around you living a consumption-driven lifestyle and reaping the delicious fruits of materialism. You see how the people you grew up with and those you went to school with spend their earnings as if there was no tomorrow. That's the point in my journey where I too began to struggle tremendously. I noticed how people in my same age group began upgrading their cars or even started building the most beautiful houses. In short, they were simply living the good, materialistic life. At the same time, I realized that they would probably never reach true financial independence during their lifetime. Luckily, my desire to reach a certain level of financial freedom kept me going through this difficult time. Even though it was a quite difficult stage, my motivation was high enough to keep walking on the path towards financial independence.

One realization that helped me to keep going was that my own desires (and other people's as well) were boundless. As time progressed, I began to understand that once I had fulfilled a certain desire for a material possession (or a certain experience that is), many other needs, wishes, urgings, and desires would emerge. Even worse, the fulfillment I experienced from purchasing something began to decline every single time after a certain while, making room for new objects of desires. This was the essential insight that made me realize what a vicious circle I found myself in. After many years of thoughtless consumption, I reflected upon my behavior and realized that not many of the things I purchased had increased my level of happiness drastically. For this reason, I slowly began to understand why they say that only those that desire little are truly rich.

As I grew older, I became a lot more experienced when it came to evaluating the opportunities that I could use my money for (e.g.

spending it or investing it). I gradually became less interested in the net worth of objects and became more interested in the passive income a certain object could generate. In general, I more and more began to differentiate between assets that could help me to earn passive income and liabilities that wouldn't earn me anything. Naturally, I gradually tried to increase the number of assets while simultaneously reducing the number of liabilities. The years went by and I suddenly noticed that I no longer saw a shiny sports car driving next to me but instead saw a piece of (beautifully designed) metal that did not earn any passive income but instead depreciates about 60% of its value within the first five years. To put it bluntly, I realized that it's an ingenious money-burning machine. Even more so, I no longer saw a successful person riding next to me in an expensive sports car. Instead, began to understand the great sacrifices this person needed to make to be able to finance such a lifestyle. In many cases, these people have an above average income but seldom have to time to enjoy the fruits of their work. Instead, they have to rush from one stressful day at work to the next, just to be able to maintain their high standard of living.

The third misconception about financial independence is that people underestimate the importance of time and how it can help them to gradually increase their savings, even if they can only contribute a small amount each year. It's a dangerous trap that I also found myself in. When you're inside it, you think that taking small but continuous steps towards financial independence is not going to be effective, which is why you leave it altogether. But when it comes to living financially free, every step you can take is important, no matter how small it seems to be. Even more so, the earlier you start working towards financial freedom, the greater the effect of compound interest, which makes it easier for you to attain financial independence.

Let's say you wish to retire at the age of 65 with $500,000 in savings. If you had started at the age of 16, you would only have to save $145 each month (until the age of 65) in order to accomplish this goal, assuming an interest rate of 6% annually. This sounds pretty feasible, doesn't it? But if you start 11 years later at the age of 27, you would already have to save $290 each month to reach your aim. So far, saving something in between $150 and $300 each month may be quite manageable, especially when you're young and without major financial responsibilities. However, a person that only begins at the age of 45 would have to save a little less than $1100 each month in order to meet the desired goal. But as we all know, a person of that age has a lot more financial responsibilities and possibly needs to take care not only for their children but also their future education. That's why it is so important to start early and to be willing to take one step after the other, no matter how small it seems initially.

As you can see from all in the above, the major obstacles lie in not knowing exactly what financial independence is, thinking that one needs to earn astronomical figures, being unwilling to reduce one's spending, and also an underestimation of the importance of time.

I hope the above has introduced you to a new perspective and different ways of thinking about financial freedom. And always remember that earning a lot of money may be one way to become financially independent, but it is only one path of many others. Whatever path towards financial freedom you choose, always follow it with the greatest determination and be willing to stick to it until you've reached your destination.

Vidya Sury

After more than a decade in the corporate world in sales/marketing/training, Vidya Sury quit her job at 33, and said bye-bye to her career when she met her soulmate to focus on family. She now enjoys the best of both worlds, living her dream as a writer/blogger/editor—writing content for clients, blogging for businesses and editing manuscripts for publishers/authors.

Today, with six blogs of her own and published contributions across the web (The Huffington Post, PTPA, World Of Moms, BlogAdda, Parentous) and as a featured Top 100 personal development blogger, she writes to collect smiles and donate to charities. She shares stories about all the things she enjoys in life—parenting, mindful living, conversations, coffee, books, food, music, health, DIY, travel, photography and showing her diabetes who's boss. Connect with her at http://vidyasury.com.

Outside the Comfort Zone is Where the Magic Happens!

The year was 1997.

At the ripe old age of 33, I handed in my resignation at work, quitting a high profile corporate job as Regional Manager with a UK-based company to get married to the most wonderful man on earth. I then relocated to his city, thinking that I would return to work after a brief sabbatical.

My Mom also came to stay with us at my husband's insistence and life was good. I was taking a break for the first time in years—I was so used to the classic busman's holiday that I had forgotten what it was like to take a real vacation.

Life was good. But I was so accustomed to being so busy that two months later, I contemplated returning to work. The motivation was an invitation from the company I had worked with. They had an opening in the city I had moved to. Just as I was on the verge of making my decision, I discovered I was pregnant, and my folks convinced me that going to work could wait. It was not so hard to agree.

In November 1997, I was blessed with a baby boy, and our family's happiness knew no bounds. I don't mind confessing that the sun shone brighter each time he smiled, and I must tell you that he was a baby who smiled all the time.

A year passed.

I once again started toying with the idea of getting back to work, but was too happy playing with my son and his toys, and enjoying life.

"Into each life must some rain fall"

All good things must come to an end, at least temporarily and so it was with our lives.

Suddenly, my Mother's health started deteriorating. She was coughing her life away, or so it seemed. She suffered for six months before the doctors reached a firm diagnosis. She had interstitial lung disease. The doctors told us that she would live for 6 months, maybe a year at most.

Naturally, we were devastated by this news. As the medical expenses steadily mounted and we struggled to keep up, I realized it was time get a job.

The thought of a second income was sensible. After all, I had a growing baby, and babies are expensive. Hospital expenses were mounting. Yet my instinct told me I should stay at home at least until my son started playschool. I consoled myself, thinking that it was only a matter of another year. But I couldn't stop worrying.

In 1999, when my son was a year and a half, we relocated again when my husband changed jobs.

Life was tough. We invested in an apartment that exceeded our budget but it was the right decision to take at that time. We were drowning in loans.

Between hospital visits and a child growing quickly, I was now job-hunting desperately so we could breathe a little easier with our financial constraints. I knew I could no longer afford to put off finding that job!

My job search was near futile, what with the job market being in a slump. It was that phase when call centers mushroomed, and employed only freshers. Of the jobs that did seem suitable, I was either overqualified or "too old". One interviewer actually told me that I was perfect for the position, but it would be embarrassing for the CEO I would be reporting to, since he was ten years younger. This did not bother me, nor did it make sense that it should matter. Nevertheless, I didn't get the job.

After a sixteen-year career that spanned advertising, sales, marketing and training, and a six-figure salary, I was miserable over my current plight, and desperate. Money was so tight, and we spent sleepless nights balancing our scarce finances.

We did everything we could to cut down on our expenditure. Other than the essentials for our toddler son and my Mom's health expenses, we lived austerely. There were days we just scraped through. Costs were rising, and soon our son would have to be enrolled in school. We silently panicked, wondering if we had been foolish in assuming that I would find a job at will, and whether we had made a mistake in investing in this apartment we lived in.

Overnight, life had changed.

Ironically, the organization I had quit before I got married offered me the same position I had held, as marketing head for the State. It hurt to decline their offer, since the job involved intense travel, late hours and a long commute. I certainly did not want to miss seeing my son growing up or be unavailable for my Mom when she needed me most.

While I battled with my dilemma, my friends advised me to accept the high-paying job offered to me on a plate—and hire a housekeeper. My head said yes, but my heart said no.

We were struggling to manage our finances, trying to be as creative as we could, to make ends meet.

As we came closer to being broke, we began to liquidate the few investments we had made, so we could pay the bills. Our savings dwindled. We spent sleepless nights, worrying about how to cut down on our expenses. We had our home loan payments to make, along with other monthly commitments.

What were we going to do?

When would things improve?

My successful sixteen-year career and the six-figure income I had given up seemed to taunt me all the time. I was slowly becoming frantic.

To rub it in, I had ex-colleagues I was in touch with telling me I was an idiot to pass up the work opportunities that came my way. And I am ashamed to say that I allowed the nagging to get to me. I felt dejected.

Inadequate. Worthless. Guilty. And hopeless.

It is all very well to talk about focusing on the silver lining, but it takes more than that to pay the bills.

Life brought unexpected changes and threw curveballs at speeds that were hard to keep up with.

I had to find the courage to let go of expectations, opening myself up to new things and recognizing what I was capable of.

To keep my mind busy, I enrolled for a training and development diploma, hoping that the additional qualification would open up more opportunities for me. I had experience in sales and communication training and somewhere at the back of my mind was the germ of an idea. What if I could work as a freelance trainer?

And then two things happened.

I got a call from a company that was looking for freelance trainers. Sounded like the answer to my prayers, right? I eagerly applied and got a 5-day gig as a soft skills trainer. That was it. They decided to "diversify" into technical coaching, which meant the end of that prospect for me.

Back to square one, I wondered what to do.

A week later, opportunity knocked.

We heard through a family friend that a friend of hers wanted someone to work part-time at their office. The pay was more like an honorarium. But determined to see the bright side, I took the job. It fit in with my son's playschool timings. I could drop him there on my way to work and pick him up on my way back home.

The office was within walking distance from my place, which meant no difficult commute and no spending on transportation. I was confident that I was close enough to rush over to my place should there be an emergency.

Although I accepted the job. My ego rebelled. I quelled it. At least it got me out of the house for a few hours, as my Mom pointed out. It made me feel employed.

Eventually, the organization grew in size, and I became their India Liaison for a consortium of US based companies that imported pharmaceuticals into the US. Slowly the role became full time, even though the money was still negligible.

In the meantime, I had ex-colleagues pointing out how stupid I was. Some were very nice. Some not so nice. Needless to say, somewhere inside me, the restlessness increased. I felt unhappy. I felt guilty. I felt inadequate.

There were days I wanted to quit my low-paying job, but I was afraid of being unemployed, because I did not have any other avenues for a steady income, and did not want to lose what little I earned.

In the meantime, the situation at home got worse at home. My Mother's health failed. She was in and out of hospital. I finally worked up the courage to tell my employers that I was quitting. Not only were they kind, but insisted that I handled one arm of the business from home. At the same salary. If only I had quit earlier, I thought, but who knew?

This was 2004, and for about a year and a half, I worked out of home for the same company. My son had started going to school.

Another year passed. During this time, many things happened.

I bought a computer at 41. Can you imagine?

The internet came into my life. That opened up a world of possibilities.

I explored work from home opportunities available at the time. After all, I had had a good career before, and was depressed that I was not bringing home the kind of money I used to.

Data entry looked lucrative as a work from home opportunity, but they asked for a hefty deposit, so that was out of the question.

I considered network marketing, but I didn't seem cut out for that kind of business.

I had often been told that my writing skills were good. I enjoyed writing stories and poetry, and had published quite a few with good reviews. I edited the in-house magazines where I worked. My grasp of idiomatic English was good. So, I thought - why not check it out?

I opened my mind and heart.

And Universe responded.

A friend asked if I would like to be a writer/editor for a business magazine, where he was co-editor. One feature article made me more than a month's salary at my current job. I had an enjoyable two months working—gasp!—as a freelance writer.

Unfortunately, the guy who funded the magazine decided to explore other investment opportunities and abandoned the project.

But this got me thinking—why not explore more freelancing opportunities?

I joined a couple of social networking sites and mentioned I was looking for freelance writing work on my profile.

On the second day, someone contacted me on MySpace, asking for writing samples. I responded right away, got accepted, and began to receive regular work. The money was still not great, but at least I had steady work, and they were good people to work with, and paid on time. I will always be grateful to them for getting me started in a tough industry

In addition, my ex-boss at the company I had worked with invited me to be part of an independent ethics committee he was setting up. The committee would meet once a week and among other responsibilities, we evaluated protocols for human clinical trials. It paid an honorarium, but I was happy to join the group of people who had been nice to me at a tough time in my life. Also, the work was enjoyable. Of course, I did not mind the pocket money, since every little helped!

I still wasn't making a full time income working from home as a freelancer. I needed to have better paying gigs.

Another challenge I faced was with time management. Working from home can be very distracting if one is not disciplined. I still had a growing son who was now in school. There were phases when Mom had to visit the hospital frequently, and I had housework to take care of.

I still got good job offers—offers I couldn't afford to take up, or lose. I just ended up feeling sad about letting go of the chance to earn big money. Sure, it made me feel marketable, but I cannot deny the twinge of regret, and that hurt.

However, life is a great teacher and I learned that if we want something, and put in the effort, everything is possible. I am happy that I had the courage to walk into something completely different and make it work.

Things work when you do

Life went on. I worked hard, hoping for that big break, that dream gig I would enjoy doing, while being paid generously. I am good at fantasizing! I kept my eyes open.

I had a steady stream of work from the agency I worked with. Didn't really pay well, but the volume made up to an extent. It also meant I had to keep slogging to earn a reasonable income. At the back of my mind lurked a feeling of gloom—I loved to write, but did not enjoy the kind of work I got. I did it anyway because I needed the money.

Then something happened that literally turned my life around.

I received an email from a prospective client via LinkedIn, asking if I would be interested in blogging for their business. I didn't really want to work with them as I knew the organization and they didn't have a good record for paying on time. I decided to put them off by quoting what I then thought was an exorbitant price for a blog post: $100. Two minutes later, pat came the response. They agreed.

I couldn't help but laugh—I mean, look at me! I was working regular gigs at an average $10 per blog post, and here I was, being crazy and keeping off a client ready to pay ten times the rate for the same work! What was wrong with me?

Fortunately, good sense prevailed. I took up the job. To my surprise, I enjoyed the work tremendously and got the first draft approved. I sent in my invoice and was quite pleased to receive my payment promptly.

I couldn't help thinking how 80% of my time was currently going into earning 20% of my income. I realized it was time to re-focus on attracting better paying work and in short—spending 20% of my time in work that brought in 80% of my income.

I mean, I *had* worked in the corporate world and taught this, so why was I not practicing what I had preached?
I was obviously blinded by the haze of self-doubt!

I cannot overemphasize the value, and importance, of believing in yourself, here. Don't assume that it is impossible to be paid what you are worth. There are enough naysayers out there, not to forget that Inner Critic ever ready inside our heads to sow those seeds of doubt and water them constantly. Even peers will laugh at you when you express your expectations. Take all that advice with a pinch of salt. In short, do not hesitate to ASK.

I know how it is. We often get so used to the routine, that we unwittingly open the door to disappointment, and get stuck in a rut. In my case, I was too used to that successful career, excelling at what I did. So when nothing seemed to work, I freaked out and grabbed at straws without pausing to think clearly. It was a matter of survival.

But you know what they say, better late than never. Luckily for me, it was sooner than later, and energized by this windfall, I forged ahead, with new hope.

Enthusiasm alone is not enough, though, as I found out. I almost believed that Universe must conspire to connect me with the right people.

It did.

It also taught me that I must set intentions and goals.

I did.

The harder I worked, the luckier I got!

I will always treasure the constant encouragement my Mom and husband gave me during these years. They always made me believe I could do whatever I set my mind to do. Except, I was not always convinced I was enough. Disappointment can cloud our thinking, creating a wall around us, preventing us from seeing the sunshine of opportunity.

I am glad to say I am not the kind of person who gives up. I am also ready to try new things. This is partly thanks to my Mom who fed me a steady diet of philosophy with her excellent cooking. She'd say, "Nothing is impossible. How can you even know the outcome of something if you don't keep an open mind? Be flexible. Be ready to change."

I now realized I had outgrown the content marketing agency I had been working with for almost 7 years now. I had discovered that it was possible to do work I enjoyed, *and* be paid well for it. Not really an epiphany and certainly not for want of trying . . . still! However, the good times had taken their own sweet time to roll in.

I did three things that transformed my working style, and this would eventually impact my finances positively. I made a list of things I wanted to do, the kind of work I was interested in. This included writing, blogging for businesses, editing manuscripts for publishers and revamping content for blogs and websites.

I hesitantly put out feelers towards direct clients.

I amped up my LinkedIn profile. Not the greatest example of what one should be, but definitely better than before. I listed the skills through which I wanted prospective clients to approach me.

This exercise alone was therapeutic. While I continued to work with the content marketing agency, work from independent clients began to trickle in. This was very exciting. Not because of the money at this point, since I wasn't making a lot, yet, but because it opened doors I had not considered before.

Almost instantly, I had people get in touch with me with work offers. Not all of it was suitable, but I did meet a few good clients whose work I enjoyed and it opened up a world of possibilities.

I also proactively started contacting publishing houses. I did a number of editing tests but the pricing was too low, so an opening was not on the immediate horizon. Editing manuscripts is very time consuming and happens over several weeks in close coordination with the author, and I simply could not afford to devote 80% of my time to 20% of my income. There I go again, with the 80-20 fetish!

Blogging

Another activity that kept me busy around the time I started working as a freelance writer was blogging. Although I started my first blog in 2003 when Google acquired Blogger, I only took it seriously when a couple of prospective clients contacted me via my blog.

Like a million others, I too dreamed of making a full time income from blogging but did not know how. Also, when I did the research, I realized I would need to invest time, a luxury I did not have.

Starting 2008, I began writing on my blog regularly, paying attention to what I posted. I consciously spent time connecting with my community, visiting other blogs, sharing their content on social media and attending blogger meets.

My first sign of recognition came when a major blogging network got in touch with me. They wanted to interview me. I agreed, of course. The exposure was welcome.

By this time, I had started my second blog—a health blog. My Mom was going through serious health issues and I felt the need for an outlet to share the knowledge I gained. At the best of times, doctors' visits are never fun. But when you come off feeling none the wiser, and have to turn to Dr.Google to clear doubts, something has to give. In my case, it was the birth of my health blog.

Lesson? No effort goes waste. And every experience teaches something.

So it looks like a nice success story, eh?

It would have been, but for the shock of my Mom suddenly passing away in February 2010, a day before my wedding anniversary. Life suddenly seemed to come to a standstill. Her death was unexpected and it shook me up emotionally. I found it hard to focus on anything other than the unavoidable routine of cooking, cleaning, eating, sleeping, and caring for my son, who was only 12.

The days passed, and I knew I had to snap out of this inertia, this listless phase. I missed my Mom terribly. I missed her encouragement and humor. I had no one to talk to. That's when I started my third blog, a sort of tribute/memoir of life with my Mom and conversations with her. This helped me cope, and get back on my feet. It also encouraged me to focus on all the loving advice I had received from my Mom and I limped back into my work routine.

This time around, though, my main goal was not money. Instead, I decided I would earn to support welfare homes, children who had no means for getting an education, schools for the blind and other charity homes.
I worked hard. I appreciated life. Work was steady. Life seemed good. Little did I know there was another shock waiting for me around the corner.

A major health setback

It was February 2013. I wanted to do something memorable that my Mom would be proud of. I decided to go for a master health check. When my lab test results came back, it shook my world up. Imagine my shock at discovering I was diabetic!

I went through a plethora of emotions. Despair followed anger, denial and despondency. I thought of all the diabetics I knew, and I so **did not** want a life like that—always worried about what I ate, and developing all sorts of complications.

But continuing to feel dejected wasn't going to get me anywhere, and so I pulled up my mental big girl panties and got to work.

For a start, I got another round of tests done, along with the blood sugar average, HbA1c, which confirmed that I was indeed a type 2 diabetic. I talked to my best friend who is a Chef to work out a diet plan. I scheduled an appointment with an endocrinologist who put me on medication. I made an exercise regime, and changed my lifestyle overnight.

In 15 days, I achieved normal blood sugar readings, but with diabetes, that was a temporary victory. The challenge was to sustain it. I took this as a wakeup call. After all, I was 50 and at the right age to focus on conscious healthy living. It was initially taxing, but I stayed focused.

Three years on, I do slip up occasionally, but I am more or less successful in showing my diabetes who's boss. I am determined to live healthy for as long as I live. And of course I want to see my son successfully complete college, settle into work he enjoys . . . I am a Mom, after all! I have dreams of traveling the world, too.

It may sound funny, but I started two more blogs at this point: one to share tips on living with diabetes, and the second to share life hacks for happiness that make life just a little better.

In life, coincidences are rare. I am included to believe that incidents happen for a reason, and exactly when they are meant to happen. When we embrace these experiences, and follow through with action, life is good.

One of the things I consistently enjoy is blogging. And in 2012, prompted by my sister and best friend, Vanita Cyril, I moved my blogs to self-hosted WordPress. Pretty much like buying your own house, and an investment well worth it. Some significant benefits I enjoy, thanks to blogging, are:

Participating in blogger outreach programs that have opened up new avenues for income. This includes sponsored posts, product and service reviews.

The ability to point prospective clients to my blogs and other published work, when they ask for writing samples.

Direct contact with brands and PR agencies for sponsored campaigns that include product reviews, both on my blogs and on social media.

Invitations from invite-only influencer marketing sites for a steady stream of sponsored content.

Recognition as an award winning blogger, with my three oldest blogs being chosen as winners in their respective categories by major blogging networks' blogging awards.

A love for books and publishing book reviews resulting in being contacted by authors and publishers for book reviews, besides helping me approach publishing houses for proofreading and copyediting manuscripts, one of my income sources today.

Invitations to contribute to several published anthologies.

Being featured in a number of Top 100 lists in the personal development, entrepreneur, mom blogger and various other niches and this has helped build connections.

Invitations to contribute on global sites like The Huffington Post, and parenting hubs such as World of Moms, PTPA and many more.

Having my content syndicated on major portals.

Invitations to participate in expert roundup posts almost every day. It is humbling to have people approach you like that!

Interviews on popular sites.

Being viewed as a kind, happy person who is always ready to help them out. I mention this because community matters in the field of blogging.

Friendships—no matter how successful one becomes, relationships matter. I've made some great friends online.

And at the core of it all, the activity that triggered all the above, writing? I have a steady income going on this, thanks to loyal and referral clients. I am also working on publishing my own non-fiction books whose drafts I am working on.

Here I must make special mention of a relationship born out of blogging, because no success story where I play the lead would be complete without her.

It was a very special day in my life when I connected with Vanita Cyril via her blog over four years ago; although I'd swear I've known her all my life.

Her support is invaluable, priceless. She is my mentor, my coach, my encourager, all rolled into one. She generously shares her expertise and resources with me, and I'd say she's responsible for many good things in my life.

She was there to lift me up when I sulked over being diagnosed with diabetes, a life-changing event as far as I am concerned. She gave excellent advice when I was at a crossroads over blogging.

I think, if every woman was blessed with a "BFF" like her, there's no limit to the heights she can rise to. Vanita and I have adopted each other and cherish our sisterhood. She's honest, outspoken, always has my back. If I had to describe her in one line, I'd say she's the kind of person who would teach a man to fish so he can feed himself for a lifetime rather than give him a fish that would feed him for a day. That's unconditional love of the highest order!

A blessed life

Today, I feel privileged to be able to give back, by doing a lot of gratis work and donating my blogging income to my local welfare home, supporting blind children's education and sharing food/education/medical expenses for orphanages, in addition to child sponsorships.

I have also been fortunate to connect with a good financial professional to invest wisely and manage my money.

I have indeed come a full circle, from starting my career as a trainee back in 1984, to rapidly rising as a corporate executive, to retiring early and then, having the courage to return to work as a freelancer.

During this emotional journey, it has been a rollercoaster ride with ups and downs, highs and lows. But I learned quite a few things about myself—and also that I can achieve anything I set my mind to!

Some lessons that have stayed with me during the years are:

- Always keep learning
- Set goals, but be flexible to change
- Explore opportunities regularly
- Consistency matters
- Give yourself credit for your talents
- Allow your family and friends to encourage you
- Ask for help when you need it. Alone you can do a lot of things, but together, so much more
- Find a mentor
- Network, network, network
- Give back
- Give without expectations
- Practice gratitude
- Make self-care part of your routine
- Learn to say No
- Learn to say Yes
- Value your time. Practice time-management
- Break free from the mold

- Don't undervalue yourself
- It is okay to be vulnerable
- Take risks. Dare to do
- Don't complain. Take action
- There is no such thing as failure
- Fear is the key to the door of opportunities

Outside the comfort zone is where the magic happens.

If I can, so can you! Today, my bio says:

After more than a decade in the corporate world in sales/marketing/training, Vidya quit her job at 33, and said bye-bye to her career when she met her soulmate, to focus on family. She now enjoys the best of both worlds, living her dream as a writer/blogger/editor—writing content for clients, blogging for businesses and editing manuscripts for publishers/authors.

Today, with six blogs of her own and published contributions across the web, she writes to collect smiles and donate to charities. She shares stories about all the things she enjoys in life; parenting, mindful living, conversations, coffee, books, food, music, health, DIY, travel, photography and showing her diabetes who's boss. Connect with her at http://vidyasury.com

Things work when you do. Believe in yourself.

Whether you think you can or think you can't, you're right!

Afterword

What a beautiful note to leave on, don't you think?

"Whether you think you can or think you can't, you're right!"

You said it best, Vidya – a Henry Ford classic.

Thanks so much to all of the co-authors who worked so hard to make this book a success. And we could not have done it without all of the awesome readers who wanted to create a better life for themselves.

This book project has been a testimony to what can be accomplished if you set your mind to it.

In closing, I want to share with you a bit about the process of putting this collaboration together.

The journey for me was in many ways a microcosm of the larger journey to financial freedom.

It was several months ago when I took Buck Flogging's List Building for Authors course. I'm not exactly an author, but I thought that the course would help me deepen my understanding of internet entrepreneurship.

That it did.

In the course, Buck proposed this book collaboration model. And for months I toyed with the model, coming up with ideas and then scrapping them.

It had been slightly over a year since I had achieved financial independence for myself. Before that, I was working job after job, gig after gig, trying desperately to support my family without having to work a traditional job.

For nearly five years of failure after failure, I had learned a set of skills that allowed me to work from home doing things that I enjoyed doing.

However, there was something missing: I had been spending my time and energy bringing others' dreams and visions to life, not my own.

I needed a model of financial independence that allowed me to be truly free: one in which I could make even more money bringing my *own* visions to life.

This book collaboration was the perfect fit.

So, naturally, I went all-in.

I'd like to say that the only thing I had to lose was time. But that wouldn't be true.

The truth is, I sacrificed so much of my current lifestyle in order to bring this vision to life.

I gave up thousands of dollars in client contracts. I abandoned everything that I had worked so hard for over the last five years, just so that I could have a shot at true financial freedom.

In the several months before launching this book project, I was only making about $800 dollars per month. Living a lifestyle that's far beyond my means was what allowed me to take what most people would consider a huge risk.

But, to me, life is about going after what you want…at all costs.

Perhaps I'm a bit impatient. But I believe that my time on this planet is precious. I refuse to spend even one day if it's not fulfilling me or helping me grow.

This project was not only fulfilling, but an immense growth experience.

I was happy to trade a handful of sleepless nights to shove this vision forward.

I was happy to drastically reduce my earnings to bring life into this project.

And I was determined to overcome all the obstacles that would emerge along the way.

So much of myself went into creating this project. Nothing was outsourced and everything was done by my own two hands, all while working out of a 1988 fifth wheel living in a junkyard in Southern Oregon.

I built the landing page, created the sales funnel, designed the cover, formatted the book, and performed 100% the outreach with nothing but a laptop and a simple idea.

Mind you, I did all this without sacrificing the relationship with my family. Nor do I believe that you ever have to sacrifice the things that are most important to you, like your health or your quality of life.

Entrepreneurship today requires nothing but your spare time, a desire to learn, and a willingness to fail.

And unlike the other 90% of times when I attempted something and failed…this time, I was ready for the failure. I was prepared to make enormous sacrifices, only to end up with yet another failure.

Before embarking on this project, I decided that a 'success' would mean simply publishing a book that featured the autobiographical stories of 15 financially free entrepreneurs.

Although I was well aware of the massive benefits and earnings potential of this project, I realized for the first time that success is never guaranteed.

That's what makes it so elusive…

…but also so beautiful.

Because I knew that if I could bring 15 people together and inspire them to share their stories, I knew that I would grow in ways that I couldn't even comprehend.

Just like with everyone who attempts to do something they've never done, I grappled with what seemed like a never-ending stream of limiting beliefs.

I do not exaggerate when I say that all of my demons came to attack me throughout the course of creating this book collaboration.

"You're not good enough," they said.

"You're a nobody. Who would ever share their stories with *you*?"

"You know you're going to fail, right?"

"You're pathetic…who do you think you are? Why don't you just go back and get a job?"

"You're worthless…no one cares about your stupid vision."

"You're going to be a failure your whole life. You'll go broke and have to move back in with your parents. And everyone will laugh at how pathetic you are."

The voices were so loud at times…it was unbelievable. There was even one night when I swear I literally saw the "evil" version of myself leave my body, float about six feet away, turn around, and laugh right in my face…all while reminding me how much of a loser I was for even trying.

It got so intense that all I could do was laugh. The fear was so much that my whole body trembled.

It didn't help to explain to myself that the reactions I was having didn't actually make a whole lot of rational sense.

What did help were the many stories I had heard about other people experiencing the same things, only to overcome their doubts and limitations and eventually achieve what they had set out to do.

The journey of creating this book collaboration was very much in line with Mahatma Gandhi's quote, "First they ignore you, then they laugh at you, then they fight you, then you win."

Only in this case, "they" were my own inner demons…perhaps the biggest, loudest, and scariest critics of all.

Throughout the creation of this project, I experienced many emotions, from shame, guilt, fear, anxiety, stress, and even some mild depression. Sure, there was some hope and excitement, but the vast majority of my experience is what most people would label "negative" emotion.

This project was so far outside of my comfort zone…but I was able to take on the challenge because I was so incredibly familiar with the demons of doubt. I had read and heard so many stories of people just like me overcoming challenges just like mine.

And that's why I decided to create this book…to give readers an inside glimpse of the journeys people have taken in order to let them know they're not alone.

Everyone has doubts. Everyone has failures. Everyone has uncertainty.

But just knowing this is enough to help get you over that edge when times get tough.

In short, this is the book I wish I had when I was starting out.

Because when I began my journey, I was a skill-less, narcissistic, arrogant, know-it-all who actually knew little to nothing about business or how the world works.

My friends and family thought I was nuts five years ago for quitting my job with no plan and no clue how to go about forming one.

But it was that insanity that allowed me to not take my circumstances so seriously.

And it was that insanity that gave me the confidence to even attempt this book project.

Any intelligent person could have pointed out the endless list of reasons why I was going to fail…and why I was a fool to even try.

I reached out to something like 20 people before I even got my first "yes."

At first, every "no" really hurt. But I simply reminded myself that for every "no," I was one step closer to a "yes."

I could have easily taken those first 20 refusals as a sign that I should give up. I could have easily taken a look at the "very real" circumstances that this was a failure.

But because of the first-hand testimonials of successful people who experienced and overcame massive rejection, I knew not to give up on my vision.

In total, I ended up reaching out to 310 successful internet entrepreneurs before I managed to get just 15 "yes's."

That's a 4.8% success rating.

By every metric or standard, that means I'm a 95.2% failure.

The truth is, if you want something in life…expect to fail the vast majority of the time. That just goes without saying.

Instead of getting down on yourself for failing, embrace each failure as a chance to get back up.

To me, the performance of this book is irrelevant. I was willing to fall simply for the opportunity to practice getting back up.

Building the confidence and courage to get back up has been the most rewarding aspect of this project.

I wouldn't trade that experience for the world.

Thanks to all those who helped turn my crazy vision into a crazy awesome reality.

Blessings to each and every one of you.

Sincerely,

Dustin Rusbarsky

P.S. The journey is not over! For more great resources on financial freedom and lifestyle design, go to www.WindingRoadtoFreedom.com. See you there!

www.ingramcontent.com/pod-product-compliance
Lightning Source LLC
Chambersburg PA
CBHW071414180526
45170CB00001B/95